The Mystery of Death

Reflections on the Spiritual Tradition

Jean Donovan

Paulist Press
New York/Mahwah

D0150224

Book design by Lynn Else
Cover design by Valerie Petro

Library of Congress Cataloging-in-Publication Data

Donovan, Jean.
    The mystery of death : reflections on the spiritual tradition / Jean Donovan.
        p. cm.
    Includes bibliographical references.
    ISBN 0-8091-4127-2 (alk. paper)
    1. Death—Religious aspects—Catholic Church. I. Title.
    BT825 .D66 2003
    236'.1—dc21

                                                        2003004577

Published by Paulist Press
997 Macarthur Boulevard
Mahwah, New Jersey 07430

www.paulistpress.com

Printed and bound in the
United States of America

Contents

Preface

For her sixth birthday, my daughter Bridget received an ant farm. Actually, what came in the box was a kit to build the ant farm and a certificate to send away for the ants. Charles, my son of nine years, was quite confident that he knew all that was necessary to begin. The kit consisted of a plastic rectangular box, slim and tall, with a plastic green tree and farm house suspended on a ledge within the box. Charles proceeded to pour sand into the box, filling the area up to the ledge. He took a straw and dug a tunnel, which he said the ants would need. There was a little tube of ant food and a syringe for water.

Several weeks went by, and finally the ants arrived. Bridget, Charles, Kathryn (my other daughter), and I sat together and opened the package. The ants were inside a small tube. It was obvious that most of them were dead. There were twenty or so shriveled up ant bodies, and perhaps ten other ants still moving. This posed our first problem. I suggested to the kids that perhaps we should put all of the ants into the ant farm. My theological background provoked me to wonder whether the ants would be aware enough of one another, and care enough about one another, to want to bury their dead. The kids agreed that it was the right thing to do. And so, very carefully, I transferred all of the ants into the ant farm.

The next morning we discovered that the dead ants had all been moved down a long plastic tube that connected one side of the ant farm to the other side. During the night the ants had begun to dig paths through the sand, and as the days went by the web of paths grew. The dead ants were moved again, this time into a pile of discarded sand. But things were not well in this ant farm. Two or three ants died. First, they stood still, appearing to be asleep. Then it became clear that they would never move again. Slowly they shriveled into black shells. Within a week or two there were only three ants left.

The kids and I did not talk very much about what was happening. Sometimes I would just sit down in front of the ant farm and stare at it. I would reread the directions, hunting for clues. The directions listed overwatering and overfeeding as potential hazards. But creatures such as ants have natural instincts that control their appetites, so these explanations seemed unjustifiable.

Finally, the kids and I dealt with the fact that something was very wrong with the ant farm and soon we would lose them all. I had an overwhelming sense of sadness when we found the last ones dead. I felt responsible, a demi-god running a puppet farm of living creatures, and a powerless one at that, because they were all dead. And I wondered whether the ant farm was the story of human life, as well.

Do we live in an ant farm? Do we struggle, working hard trying to build a life for ourselves and our families, only to watch it all fall apart and decay? As we bury our dead, are we just moving their bodies from one place to another, where finally we will find ourselves as well? Is there something more to life for us?

Introduction

Life, ultimately, is a mystery. So is death. Does it take a long time to come to this realization? It probably depends on the person. Perhaps it begins in childhood. Child psychologists talk about children as "magicians" who wave their wands and order their worlds.[1] They realize intuitively their absolute powerlessness and seek to strike out against that reality. Anyone attempting to comfort a raging two year old can attest to the fact that sometimes they succeed.

Becoming aware of the mysteries seems to be universal to human experience. Situating our planet in the universe; failing to find life elsewhere; grappling with the complexities of human existence; experiencing the power of love and its incredible expression in the birth of children; then finding disease, strife, and death dogging the human spirit—these many realities point to the deepest mysteries of our existence.

And where is God in this life of ours? Human beings have experienced something, some presence, some guidance, some voice that calls to us. Capturing that experience is the stuff of ancient texts, poetry, and song. Human beings throughout the centuries have been aware of the mystery of life. We are caught up in a world that is infinitely larger than we are. We share the search for meaning with our ancestors and our descendants. This book is a conversation within the Christian tradition that focuses on our search for meaning, our place in the universe, and our relationship to that mystery we call God.

In a world dominated by a consumer culture and virtual reality, it seems important to begin a conversation about death as our "horizon"; on the distant shore of our lives it stands, waiting. No matter how busy our lives are, or how important our jobs, or how committed we are to family, friends, and community, there is no escape from questions of meaning. In today's society, it seems, we are touched briefly by these questions, perhaps as we mill around in the rooms of a funeral home or sit silently in the pews of a church as we go through the funeral rites. But that is, for human beings rich in intelligence and depth of perception, too little, too late. In understanding death as our horizon, we come to construct our lives with greater care. To see death frees us to know life better; it helps us to wrestle with the mystery in which we live.

The text is a conversation, not a lecture; it offers a collection of questions for meditation, not a handbook of questions and answers. When I have discussed this project over the last year or so, people occasionally respond with a raised eyebrow or a hopeful glance. It is a difficult subject to discuss, but my experience teaching college students and doing parish workshops tells me that a clear, comprehensive discussion of these topics is needed. People are wrestling with life experiences, like the death of their child, and they don't have the spiritual and pastoral resources available to help them weather what life has handed to them. College-age students probe deeply into the meaning of life and need to have solid reading materials to engage their minds and hearts. This text has been designed for them.

The text is divided into two parts. In the first part, the issues of death, suffering, accountability, and happiness are addressed. Imagine a large table, and on it 100 puzzle pieces. Your task is to assemble the puzzle. Anyone who has ever worked on a puzzle has developed certain habits for sorting and beginning the puzzle. Perhaps you find all of the straight pieces first, and then you construct the frame. Or you sort by color or image, and put together pieces that form a figure or an object. Each issue is a section of the puzzle. As you begin to read the chapter, you will find three resources: scripture references; quotations and discussions from Christians who have lived in different times in church history, some of them from the earliest days; and material from modern-day theologians. You will receive enough information in the text to help you begin to understand the issue and form your own thoughts on it, so do not feel uncomfortable or concerned if you do not have a lot of background in reading the Bible or in theology. The chapter is designed to explain things to you as you go along. However, a Bible and a good commentary on the Bible would be helpful. I recommend the *Catholic Study Bible*, along with a basic history book on the growth of Christianity from the early days in the Middle East to its growth in Western Europe and beyond, and a modern-day discussion of the Catholic Church's life and teachings. These will serve as resources for you, to aid in reading the text. I have tried, especially when using early Christian writers, to quote enough from their writings for the selections to be understandable and sufficient for your use in putting together the puzzle. Nonetheless, you might be curious or have other questions, and if you have other resources available to you, it will be helpful. Your goal for each chapter is to organize the ideas and questions in your own mind and begin to assemble them in a manner that will prepare you to complete the second part of the book. Taking notes, especially in the form of a journal, in which you record your own thoughts, impressions, memories, and responses, is a good idea, too.

As you move through the chapters, the puzzle will begin to take shape. Many of these questions are difficult to face, and the work will not be easy. Writing in your journal will become more and more important. The goal is to reach a point where you can come to a personal statement of your beliefs. Part Two of the text is an example of a personal statement for you to read. It is mine. It comes from the mix of who I am as a person; what I have learned through my years of study and research in Catholic theology; and from my experiences as a college professor, lay minister, and crisis worker. I do not expect you to take my personal statement as your own statement. It is an example of the necessary second half of this project. This particular puzzle, this puzzle about the meaning of life, will not be complete without your input. You must connect the pieces through your own statement. Otherwise, the pieces will remain unconnected and of no particular value to you.

It has been a long and interesting journey, writing this text. I have been collecting materials, thinking, and writing for five years. In some ways it is a work in progress. I am still wrestling with some things, struggling with others, but writing the personal statement brought me to a place of peace and to a sense of accomplishment. It is my hope that you will find some satisfaction in taking on the challenges set before you in this text.

PART ONE
Raising the Questions

1

Death

Why Do We Die?

Life is a mystery. And so is death. Perhaps the strangest dimension of our human experience in the face of death is the fact that we are aware of our fate. As humans, we are able to grasp the fundamental reality of our mortality long before we are ever threatened with it. The animal we see scurrying across the road or racing away from its predator can smell the danger of the moment and fights to live. We can smell death when nothing in our experience threatens us. Death begs the question of life. What does it mean to be alive? Our consciousness of ourselves evolves over time; our very nature, experience, and personality change significantly throughout the course of our life. The person we were as a child evolves into mature adulthood, and then perhaps recedes somewhat as we enter old age. The fact that we experience ourselves as autonomous, particular, and important, even though there are literally millions of other human beings, evokes the mystery; we can't see the how and why of our conscious selves, nor can we determine our destiny.

⁃ The why of death must be linked somehow with the why of life; if I know who I am, and why I am alive, I might be able to understand why I am going to die. Perhaps, though, these two questions will be answered simultaneously; in the face of death, I will come to know who I am.

Mythology is the art of storytelling, when meanings at the deepest level are shared through narratives that strike a chord within us. The ancient stories of the Old Testament are building blocks that construct the worldview of the people of Israel. Chapter 1 of Genesis tells how God created the world. First came order from chaos, then earth and sky, and sun and stars. Then God created living creatures to populate the earth.

> Then God said: "Let us make man in our image, after our likeness. Let them have dominion over the fish of the sea, the birds of the air, and the cattle, and over all the wild animals and all the creatures that crawl on the ground."

> God created man in his image;
>   in the divine image he created him;
>   male and female he created them.

> God blessed them, saying to them: "Be fertile and multiply; fill the earth and subdue it." (Gen 1:26–28)

These narratives tell the story of the origin of the human race. The people of Israel, and their Christian descendants, believe that we are created by God, made in God's own image. It is God's plan that led to the creation of the ordered universe, the cosmos, and within that plan there is a destiny etched for humanity. The extraordinary nature of the human person, which sets us apart from other creatures, is the divine spark, the image of God, within us. This was God's intention. The dreams of immortality that have fired the human race can rest upon this simple story: Made in the image of God, we are not completely bound by the limits of mortal existence. Saint Irenaeus, an early church father, in his writings against the heresies said that "we are made in God's image, but we must grow to God's likeness." This raises a question: What kind of life did God intend for humanity? And this brings our attention to another myth in the Book of Genesis: the fall. The story of Adam and Eve in the Garden of Eden portrays the origin of humanity's suffering.

According to a second creation account in Genesis, a garden was planted in Eden, where Adam and Eve were to live. "A river rises in Eden to water the garden" (Gen 2:10); that river had four branches, the Pishon, the Gihon, the Tigris, and the Euphrates. Thus the land of Eden was located in the Tigris-Euphrates river valley, known as the cradle of civilization. Adam and Eve were free to live in this garden, according to the narrative of the fall, and to eat what they wanted, with one exception: They were forbidden to eat of the fruit of the tree of the knowledge of good and evil. That proved to be a temptation they were unable to resist. Eve was coaxed by the serpent, "the most cunning of all the animals" (Gen 3:1), to eat the fruit. "The woman saw that the tree was good for food, pleasing to the eyes, and desirable for gaining wisdom. So she took some of its fruit and ate it; and she also gave some to her husband, who was with her, and he ate it" (Gen 3:6).

Upon eating, Adam and Eve suddenly become aware that they are naked, and so they cover themselves with fig leaves. God appears to them. When God discovers that they have eaten the fruit of the forbidden tree, God asks, "Why did you do such a thing?" (Gen 3:13). God metes out the severest of punishments.

To the woman he said:
   "I will intensify the pangs of your childbearing;
     in pain shall you bring forth children.
Yet your urge shall be for your husband,
     and he shall be your master."

To the man he said: "Because you listened
to your wife and ate from the tree of which I had
forbidden you to eat,

"Cursed be the ground because of you!
   In toil shall you eat its yield
   all the days of your life.

Thorns and thistles shall it bring forth to you,
  as you eat of the plants of the field.
By the sweat of your face
  shall you get bread to eat,
Until you return to the ground,
  from which you were taken;
For you are dirt,
  and to dirt you shall return." (Gen 3:16–19)

As the narrative unfolds, the destiny of the human race is altered by the failure of this primeval man and woman; their inability to comply with the strictures of life in the garden distorts human life and destiny. Punishments abound. Woven within the story lies the hint of sexuality. It is a part of the knowledge they have acquired (awareness of nakedness), as well as a part of the punishment (the woman's "urge" for her husband, presumably sexual desire, will be the trap that will allow him to have power over her; the consequences of their sexual liaison, pregnancy, will further torment her with pain at childbirth). The woman's punishment provides justification for Israel's later laws controlling women's place in society; Eve is held accountable for seducing Adam into sin, so later generations of women were presumed to be dangerous to men as well.

The man is punished with suffering and death. He must struggle to eke out a harvest from barren ground, a battle that will endure until he returns to the ground from which he came. From abundance to scarcity, from life to death, the harshness of the punishment is almost inconceivable. Why would the human race, gifted with the spark of divine nature, so quickly and permanently fall into disgrace?

The narrative ends with their banishment from the Garden of Eden. And the tree of life, which would have given them immortality, is now guarded by the "cherubim and the fiery revolving sword" (Gen 3:24) Many questions could be raised. Were Adam and Eve destined to die after life in the garden? Or were they originally to eat of the tree of life? The original ban seems only to have been from the fruit of the tree of the knowledge of good and evil. What role does sexual awakening play in the destiny of men and women? Some biblical scholars have argued that the story is simply a "coming of age" narrative, in which children naturally lose their innocence in the transition to full adulthood. And yet it seems that the punishment far exceeds the "crime" of sexual maturity.

If we return to our original question—Why do we die?—we see that the creation myths posit several things. God, the living force, created the universe and placed humanity among a variety of living creatures. In addition, the human race had dominion (cf. Gen 1:26). The question of death does not figure into the narrative until the story of the fall. Humanity sought wisdom and power, against the express will of God, and thus lost the beatific life in the Garden of Eden. [Pain, suffering, and death are the result of this disobedience. Why do we die? According to the ancient myths of the Bible, we die because we sought more than what we had a right to have and to be.]

This set of narratives poses a variety of problems. Perhaps the least difficult to work through is the time frame: the creation of the world in seven days, a human race complete from its original formation. Much more challenging are the consequences that are evoked by this primeval woman and man; their one act of disobedience destroys the entire life-giving, joy-filled wonder of creation. "God looked at everything he had made, and he found it very good. Evening came, and morning followed—the sixth day" (Gen 1:31). How could the entire enterprise of creation be sidetracked in such a miserable and permanent way?

There are other mythologies in our own times, perhaps more satisfying, perhaps less satisfying. The scientific community has presented extensive research and speculation about alternative schemes in an effort to explain both the origin of the universe and the human race. In his book *Cosmos,* Carl Sagan, internationally renowned for his work in astronomy and the American space program, tells a story about the universe and our place in it:

> Finally, at the end of all our wanderings, we return to our tiny, fragile, blue-white world, lost in a cosmic ocean vast beyond our most courageous imaginings. It is a world among an immensity of others. It may be significant only for us. The Earth is our home, our parent. Our kind of life arose and evolved here. The human species is coming of age here. It is on this world that we developed our passion for exploring the Cosmos, and it is here that we are, in some pain and with no guarantees, working out our destiny. Welcome to the planet Earth—a place of blue nitrogen skies, oceans of liquid water, cool forests and soft meadows, a world positively rippling with life. In the cosmic perspective it is, as I have said, poignantly beautiful and rare; but it is also, for the moment, unique. In all our journeying through space and time, it is, so far, the only world on which we know with certainty that the matter of the Cosmos has become alive and aware. There must be many such worlds scattered through space, but our search for them begins here, with the accumulated wisdom of men and women of our species, garnered at great cost over a million years. We are privileged to live among brilliant and passionately inquisitive people, and in a time where the search for knowledge is generally prized. Human beings, born ultimately of the stars and now for a while inhabiting a world called Earth, have begun their long voyage home.[1]

It is useful to pause for a moment and make several observations. This is mythology, as clearly as were the narratives in the Book of Genesis. It is imbued with "meaning"; it bears within it explanations based on belief as well as on evidence. For example, Carl Sagan talks about the cosmos rather than the universe. *Cosmos,* a word of Greek origin, means the ordered, meaningful universe. By his choice of word, Sagan has already committed himself to believing that the stars, galaxies, and all of space itself come together into a meaningful whole. This is not self-evident; it is a statement of belief. Sagan believes that the universe is an ordered reality.

A second observation: Sagan believes "the Earth is our home, our parent." Again, this is a mixture of fact and belief. Of course the earth is our home, but is it our parent? This statement that our relationship with the earth bears a resemblance to the intimate bond of parent and child is poetic, perhaps inspiring, certainly reminiscent of Native American spirituality, and again, a belief.

A last example: "Human beings, born ultimately of the stars." The personification of the creator as God seems parallel to this statement "born of the stars." How and why would human beings be born in this fashion? Is there some personal presence within the stars that generated this creation? Or is he attempting to use a technical term to describe the evolution of the universe? The language and imagery is poetic and evocative; it is also mythological. What explanations do we see, rising from the text? Humanity is not alone in the universe; we have simply not discovered the other worlds yet ("there must be many such worlds scattered through space"). The development of human society and knowledge has been wrought by human effort "garnered at great cost over a million years." Some level of suffering seems to be inherent in these enormous responsibilities ("it is here that we are, in some pain and with no guarantees, working out our destiny"). Sagan does not explain why pain and struggle exist in human efforts to move toward the future. Perhaps most challenging to the Genesis narratives, independent, aggressive human ambition for knowledge is praised as the great strength of the human race, rather than its most dangerous weakness ("we are privileged to live among brilliant and passionately inquisitive people, and in a time when the search for knowledge is generally prized").

Stephen Hawking, a theoretical physicist whose influence is often compared to that of Einstein, observed that the conversation among scientists about the origin and destiny of the universe has by and large been a private one.

> Up to now, most scientists have been too occupied with the development of new theories that describe *what* the is to ask the question *why*. On the other hand, the people whose business it is to ask *why*, the philosophers, have not been able to keep up with the advance of scientific theories. In the eighteenth century, philosophers considered the whole of human knowledge, including science, to be their field and discussed questions such as: Did the universe have a beginning? However, in the nineteenth and twentieth centuries, science became too technical and mathematical for the philosophers, or anyone else except for a few specialists....If we do discover a complete theory, it should in time be understandable in broad principle by everyone, not just a few scientists. Then we shall all, philosophers, scientists, and just ordinary people, be able to take part in the discussion of the question of why it is that we and the universe exist. If we find the answer to that, it would be the ultimate triumph of human reason—to know the mind of God.[2]

Hawking and his colleagues around the world are seeking a theory of "everything" that would unite what they understand about the beginning of the universe, the "Big Bang," and the principles that govern the workings of the universe. Further, David Filkin notes in his commentary on Hawking's work, *Stephen Hawking's Universe*, that there is a "mismatch between the physics of the very large (relativity) and the physics of the very small (quantum mechanics)."[3] And so more work needs to be done for human science to achieve a complete understanding of how the universe works; theoretical physicists, astrophysicists, and mathematicians focus on the how, as Hawking says, but not really the why. Much of what they have determined provokes unanswered questions, for example, the Big Bang theory:

> It is, of course, annoying that everything is not sorted out completely, leaving us with a comforting, neat, totally proven picture of the dynamics of the universe. But at least our present understanding of matter fits amazingly well with our present understanding of the way the universe has developed. All the mathematical equations can be fitted together to build an astonishingly precise picture of its evolution.
>
> It all begins with a dramatic Big Bang explosion producing nothing but searing hot energy at first. This energy somehow develops slight variations in its texture as it spreads outward and starts to cool. This allows for slightly hotter spots where, within the first second after the Big Bang, energy starts converting into particles and antiparticles; and slightly cooler spots which are destined to become the first voids in space. Most of the particles and antiparticles start to be drawn close enough together by gravity for what is known as the electromagnetic force to make them combine; and most of the antimatter is lost in annihilation, leaving only matter swirling in growing irregular clumps. Until three minutes after the Big Bang, it is still too hot for these subatomic particles to build anything together; but then some of them start to bind into what will become the nuclei of atoms. It takes 300,000 years for things to cool down enough for electrons to couple with these nuclei to form the first atoms.[4]

Filkin continues, describing the succession of events: Helium and hydrogen are first produced, but billions of years will elapse before gravity pulls them together to form galaxies, stars, and planets.

Hawking himself identifies questions that remain:

> (1) Why was the early universe so hot?; (2) Why is the universe so uniform on a large scale?;...(3) Why did the universe start out with so nearly the critical rate of expansion that separates models that recollapse from those that go on expanding forever, so that even now, ten thousand million years later, it is still expanding at nearly the critical rate?; (4) Despite the fact that the universe is so uniform and homogeneous on a large scale, it contains irregularities...Why does the universe go to all the bother of existing? Is the unified theory so compelling that it brings about its own existence? Or does it need a creator, and, if so, does he have any other effect on the universe? And who created him?[5]

Hawking plays at the notion of God in his theories. He also spends a bit of time avoiding confrontations with the Catholic Church, because, he says, he doesn't want to suffer the same fate as his predecessor Galileo.[6]

The Big Bang theory can be empirically verified, but it does not contain a self-evident cause or purpose. The theorists can experiment about the how and speculate on the why, but they have yet to eliminate the "awesome mystery" of what has happened in the creation of the universe."[7] Much the same can be said about the origin of life on earth.

According to the Big Bang theory, life can evolve if the planet has formed in the right way for it to do so.[8] Stephen Hawking, giving a lecture at the White House in anticipation of the new millennium, commented on the development of life:

By far the most complex systems we have are our own bodies. Life seems to have originated in the primordial oceans that covered the earth four billion years ago. How this happened we don't know. It may be that random collisions between atoms built up macromolecules that could reproduce themselves and assemble themselves into more complicated structures. What we do know is that by three and a half billion years ago the highly complicated DNA molecule had emerged.[9]

The story of creation woven by the theoretical physicists is as yet unfinished. They themselves are not yet satisfied; they still seek a unifying "theory of everything." But the why of it all, remains elusive.

The story of creation and the fall in the Book of Genesis, and the story of the Big Bang and the formation of DNA, provide, in their own ways, clues to the origin of the universe and of life. If we need to understand the meaning of life in order to understand the meaning of death, then the overpowering mystery of our experience will not be explained away by either.

Although it would be possible to go on collecting and discussing myths from various religious traditions, cultures, and time periods, that would lead us away from the task of exploring the meaning of life and death from a Christian perspective. So, one further myth, taken from the Christian scriptures, will be discussed: the birth of Jesus.

The angel Gabriel was sent from God to a town of Galilee called Nazareth, to a virgin betrothed to a man named Joseph, of the house of David, and virgin's name was Mary.

And coming to her, he said, "Hail, favored one! The Lord is with you." But she was greatly troubled at what was said and pondered what sort of greeting this might be. Then the angel said to her, "Do not be afraid, Mary, for you have found favor with God. Behold, you will conceive in your womb and bear a son, and you shall name him Jesus. He will be great and will be called Son of the Most High, and the Lord God will give him the throne of David his father, and he will rule over the house of Jacob forever, and of his kingdom there will be no end." But Mary said to the angel, "How can this be, since I have no relations with a man?" And the angel said to her in reply, "The holy Spirit will come upon you, and the power of the Most High will overshadow you. Therefore the child to be born will be called holy, the Son of God."...Mary said, "Behold, I am the handmaid of the Lord. May it be done to me according to your word." Then the angel departed from her. (Luke 1:26–35, 38)

The Gospel of Luke includes this infancy narrative. It makes two claims about the baby who is to be born: The child will inherit the kingdom begun with King David, leader of the people of Israel around 1000 B.C.E., and its promises; and the child will be the Son of God, born of the Spirit, not of a human father, and the woman Mary. There are other myths of divine birth in ancient cultures, but this narrative survived through the centuries as a part of the Christian tradition. It describes the origin of a dynamic force that entered into ordinary human life; claims will be made about this person Jesus, about his ability to define life and conquer death ("I am the light of the world. Whoever follows me will not walk in darkness, but will have the light of life" [John 8:12]).

In the beginning was the Word,
    and the Word was with God,
    and the Word was God.
He was in the beginning with God.
All things came to be through him,
    and without him nothing came to be.
What came to be through him was life,

and this life was the light of the human race;
the light shines in the darkness,
and the darkness has not overcome it. (John 1:1–5)

Jesus is the Word, present at creation. The Word, or Logos, seems to be the Wisdom, or Sophia, of the Old Testament tradition.[10] Sophia was "first-born," "before the earth." (Prov 8:22, 23) Solomon prays that God will send him Wisdom,

who knows your works
and was present when you made the world;...
For she knows and understands all things,
and will guide me discreetly in my affairs
and safeguard me by her glory. (Wis 9:9, 11)

According to Elizabeth Johnson, Jesus becomes, in the writings of the first century, the "embodiment of Sophia herself."[11] The Christian community experienced Jesus as the presence of God incarnate in the world. By touching the Old Testament tradition of Wisdom, early Christians saw the divine presence as Trinity, the community of the Godhead. The myths of the creation of the Christian community reveal a God involved in human history, a God who becomes human to transform life and heal human suffering.

The Christian myth of the birth of the Christ child, Jesus, is a historical claim, a unique moment in history when a human being is born who is more fully divine than any other human before him (perhaps one could say a moment in the evolution of the spiritual capacity of the human race). The fullness of divinity and humanity within Jesus gives him the name of Son of God. The Christian community draws on the rich heritage of Old Testament belief and spirituality in coming to understand the nature of this divine birth. Jesus is a Jew, born among Jews in first-century Palestine. A Roman historian, Tacitus, wrote about the Christians early in the second century:

> They got their name from Christ, who was executed by sentence of the procurator Pontius Pilate in the reign of Tiberius. That checked the pernicious superstition for a short time, but it broke afresh—not only in Judea, where the plague first arose, but in Rome itself where all the horrible and shameful things in the world collect and find a home.[12]

The myth of Jesus' divinity is constructed on the life of the person Jesus, a life that lasted a few short years, years filled with preaching, healing, and challenging the social and religious structures of his day. His life ended violently. He was arrested, accused of blasphemy, abandoned by his followers, and condemned to death by the Roman authorities. He was tortured and crucified, hung on a cross to be slowly asphyxiated, an agonizing death to which Roman citizens were never sentenced, no matter what crimes they had committed. And that would have been the end of the story had his followers not experienced his presence again. The resurrection narratives in the New Testament record their encounters with the risen Jesus:

> While they were still speaking about this, he stood in their midst and said to them, "Peace be with you." But they were startled and terrified and thought that they were seeing a ghost. Then he said to them, "Why are you troubled? And why do questions arise in your hearts? Look at my hands and feet, that it is I myself. Touch me and see, because a ghost does not have flesh and bones as you can see I have." And as he said this, he showed them his hands and his feet. While they were still incredulous for joy and were amazed, he asked them, "Have you anything here to eat?"

They gave him a piece of baked fish; he took it and ate it in front of them.

He said to them, "These are my words that I spoke to you while I was still with you, that everything written about me in the law of Moses and in the prophets and psalms must be fulfilled." Then he opened their minds to understand the scriptures. And he said to them, "Thus it is written that the Messiah would suffer and rise from the dead on the third day and that repentance, for the forgiveness of sins, would be preached in his name to all the nations, beginning from Jerusalem. You are witnesses of these things. And [behold] I am sending the promise of my Father upon you; but stay in the city until you are clothed with power from on high." (Luke 24:36–49)

The Book of Acts chronicles the early struggles of the first Christians, the coming of the Spirit, their efforts at preaching and healing as Jesus did, their missionary travels, the stoning of one of the followers, the arrest of another. And so the history goes, for two thousand years.

Why do we die? The myths of creation, of the origin of the universe and the beginning of human life, inform and respond to some extent to our questions. The stories in Genesis record the beginning of time and space with the creation of the universe by God. The mystery of God's nature and the purpose of human life are joined in the union of the physical and the spiritual. Humanity exists because God willed it into existence. The human race is laden with burdens and struggles because of its efforts to seize equality with God. To some extent modern-day scientists challenge these assumptions, most poignantly the time frame of seven days. A "singularity," a unique moment for the beginning of creation is proposed. Scientists seem confident that they can tell us the how of creation, but remain daunted by the why. And the mystery of life, and of human will and suffering, are revealed in the life of Christ. An explosion of tremendous magnitude that burns for billions of years forms a part of the mystery of life. A man named Jesus is perhaps a part of that reality as well. If life is ultimately a mystery, then death's mystery should not come as a surprise.

Why do we die? On the most basic level, the body wears down. The slow progression of aging is well documented and easily observable. The human person's life is bound by space and by time, which flows relentlessly in a linear direction; life has a beginning and an end. Reflecting on Homer's *Odyssey* and Swift's *Gulliver's Travels* on the question of death, Harold Kushner proposes that life without death would be in its own way unbearable:

> Homer shows us an immortal being envying us for being mortal. Swift teaches us to pity the person who cannot die. He wants us to realize that living with the knowledge that we will die may be frightening and tragic, but knowing we will never die would be unbearable. We might wish for a longer life, or a happier one, but how could any of us endure a life that went on forever?[13]

Perhaps death, then, is just a part of life, an aspect of existence that defines the parameters, that gives focus and closure to a life that would otherwise be adrift in a sea of experiences. Think of a parking space, so desperately important when one is circling a parking lot, rushing to catch a plane, so irrelevant when the trip is over and one is on the way home. For those who go to college, freshman year holds an excitement, an explosion out of childhood, a sense that all of life is ahead. The freedom is breathtaking. But a few short years down the road the air is stifling, and the student longs to end the relentless repetition of classes and assignments. What was once fresh and desirable becomes a tiresome burden. For those who achieve the ordinary milestones of life—growing up, education, marriage, parenting, useful employment, home and family—each stage's fulfillment brings an end to its longing, until one day all of life's ambitions have been attained. What is next?

If, as the resurrection accounts suggest, Jesus brings a new life that has conquered and transformed death, then we are drawn into the next array of questions: What happens after death? If death is a natural partner to human life, then why is it that human beings die in such pain? Why does suffering so often shadow death?

Why Do We Suffer?

In order to explore the above question fully, we need to define what we mean by *suffering*. Theologians and philosophers who write on the question often distinguish between physical pain and psychological suffering. Physical pain includes hunger and thirst, as well as disease and injury. Psychological suffering involves the mental and emotional pain of loneliness, anxiety, remorse, lack of love, fear, grief, and envy.[14] The cause of suffering, whether physical, mental, or emotional, can be attributed either to moral evil, the conscious actions of other human beings, or natural evil from fire, floods, tornados, earthquakes, hurricanes, or thunderstorms.[15] Suffering is a complex experience affecting us on many levels. Our awareness of the reality of suffering itself causes pain:

> I know there are questions that have no answers; there is a suffering that has no name; there is injustice in God's creation—and there are reasons enough for man to explode with rage. I know there are reasons for you to be angry. Good. Let us be angry. Together.[16]

Elie Wiesel is here talking about a great Hasidic spiritual leader, Rebbe Barukh of Medezebozh (1757–1811), who lived in Eastern Europe during another era of violent antisemitism;

Wiesel himself lived in our era, surviving the Holocaust. Wiesel reflects on melancholy, and the great spiritual struggles that life inflicts. Rebbe Barukh, concerned about a student who was lost in despair, seeks him out and confronts him:

"You are surprised to see me here, in your room? You shouldn't be. I can read your thoughts, I know your inner-most secrets. You are alone and trying to deepen your lone-liness. You have already passed through, one after the other, the fifty gates of knowledge and doubt—and I know how you did it.

"You began with one question; you explored it in depth to discover the first answer, which allowed you to open the first gate; you crossed it and found yourself confronted by a new question. You worked on its solution and found the second gate. And the third. And the fourth and the tenth; one leads to the other, one is a key to the other. And now you stand before the fiftieth gate.

"Look. it is open. And you are frightened, aren't you? The open gate fills you will fear, because if you pass through it, you will face a question to which there is no answer—no human answer. And if you try, you will fall. Into the abyss. And you will be lost. Forever. You didn't know that. Only I did. But now you also know."

"What am I to do?" cried the disciple, terrified. "What can I do? Go back? To the beginning? Back to the first gate?"—

"Impossible," said the Master. "Man can never go back; it is too late. What is done cannot be undone."

There was a long silence. Suddenly the young disciple began to tremble violently. "Please, Rebbe," he cried, "help me. Protect me. What is there left for me to do? Where can I go from here?"—

"Look," said Rebbe Barukh. "Look in front of you. Look beyond that gate. What keeps man from running, dashing over its threshold? What keeps man from falling? Faith. Yes, son: beyond the fiftieth gate there is not only the abyss but also faith—and they are one next to the other."[17]

We would be fools to think of suffering in the abstract, in simplistic ways. Suffering is people maimed and brutalized, starved and homeless, hated and scorned, abandoned and vilified. The worst of suffering is inflicted by one human being on another, by one tribe on another, by one race on another, by one religion on another, by one society on another. The problem of suffering is really a problem of sin. It is the problem of broken promises, empty words, loveless actions. Elie Wiesel, recounting his experiences of living in the concentration camp of Auschwitz during World War II, writes of a hanging, with one of the victims a child:

> I witnessed other hangings. I never saw one of the victims weep. For a long time those dried-up bodies had forgotten the bitter taste of tears....One day when we came back from work, we saw three gallows rearing up in the assembly place, three black crows. Roll call. SS all round us, machine guns trained: the traditional ceremony. Three victims in chains—and one of them, the little servant, the sad-eyed angel.
>
> The SS seemed more preoccupied, more disturbed than usual. To hang a young boy in front of thousands of spectators was no light matter. The head of the camp read the verdict. All eyes were on the child. He was lividly pale, almost calm, biting his lips. The gallows threw its shadow over him....The three victims mounted together onto the chairs. The three necks were placed at the same moment within the nooses....At a sign from the head of the camp, the three chairs tipped over. Total silence throughout the camp. On the horizon, the sun was setting. "Bare your heads!" yelled

the head of the camp. His voice was raucous. We were weeping. "Cover your heads!" Then the march past began. The two adults were no longer alive. Their tongues hung swollen, blue-tinged. But the third rope was still moving; being so light, the child was still alive....For more than a half an hour he stayed there, struggling between life and death, dying in slow agony under our eyes. And we had to look him full in the face. He was still alive when I passed in front of him. His tongue was red, his eyes not yet glazed. Behind me, I heard [a] man asking: "Where is God now?"[18]

Suffering is a problem of the human race. We wield the power to destroy one another. This is our first objective: to address the misery caused by human beings.

We also need to consider the pain of physical suffering, the diseases of the body that shorten our lives and make us endure pain. Perhaps evolution provides a quick path to explanation, the human race still working out the kinks, as well as poor diet, lack of exercise and addictive bad habits. We can make easy work of earthquakes and tornados, too. The wildest winds of nature, the trembling, shaking earth, bears us no malice. We can wonder why, but it does not seem to strike at our souls, tear apart our confidence in life, the way raw evil does.

Moral theologians today distinguish between *personal* sin and *social* sin. Personal sins are those actions (or omissions) that hurt oneself or others directly. Their effects are immediate. Social sins or structural sins are embedded in society itself; their effects that are felt over a long period of time by many people who may never even know the perpetrators of the original actions. Social sins include political corruption, illegal insider-trading, racial bias in the work place, segregated housing. One of the most pervasive social sins in modern society is the division between the "haves" and the "have nots"; world peace is threatened every day by the uprising of peoples who have been denied the most basic of rights and necessities. In the United States poverty, illiteracy, homelessness, and violence raise profound questions about a society based on the ideals of "life, liberty, and the pursuit of happiness."

Why do we suffer? We suffer because of hatred, envy, and selfishness. We suffer because something is "unfinished" about the life of the community. The life we should share together as families, neighbors, friends, colleagues, and citizens is a far cry from the life we know. We may be banging our head against a wall in trying to understand why evil exists. But it is clear that it does. Why do we suffer? Is suffering absurd, meaningless, or does it have a purpose?

C. S. Lewis, an Oxford scholar in literature, novelist, and Christian apologist writing at the beginning of World War II discussed the problem of pain.[19] He suggested that the notion that suffering builds character might still be valid. He pointed to Hebrews 2:9–10 and its discussion of Jesus' redemptive suffering.

> We do see Jesus "crowned with glory and honor" because he suffered death, he who "for a little while" was made "lower than the angels," that by the grace of God he might taste death for everyone.
>
> For it was fitting that he, for whom and through whom all things exist, in bringing many children to glory, should make the leader to their salvation perfect through suffering.[20]

When the innocent suffer, they grow in strength. When people endure injustice, disappointment, hardship, or tragedy, they are crystallized in the process; they become stronger, purer, more courageous. We suffer, Lewis's argument goes, because it is the path to our destiny, the full realization of our divine potential. In the struggles of life we become more than we would have been otherwise. The Christian community sees

Jesus' innocent suffering and death as a power unleashed to conquer death. Lewis also argues that pain is a punishment intended to awaken sinners, "God's megaphone" to save sinners from themselves:[21]

> When our ancestors referred to pains and sorrows as 'God's vengeance' upon sin they were not necessarily attributing evil passions to God; they may have been recognizing the good element in the idea of retribution. Until the evil man finds evil unmistakably present in his existence, in the form of pain, he is enclosed in illusion.[22]

Pain wakes us up and refocuses our energies toward the good.

Is suffering an end in itself? Lewis would say no.[23] In the early church the answer sometimes seemed to be yes. Christians idolized martyrdom. Saint Cyprian (c. 210–58), bishop of Carthage, addressed the issue of suffering, pain, and fear of death in his treatise "On the Mortality." The "mortality" he refers to is a plague that is spreading among the people. Martyrdom is also at issue. Cyprian and his followers are living in a violent era of Christian history. (Cyprian himself will die a martyr's death during the persecution of the Roman emperor Valerian.) Christians are suffering from the disease, which robs them of life just as it does the "heathens." It even robs them of the chance for the glory of martyrdom. Cyprian comforts them, saying it is not their choice, but God's, as to who is called to martyrdom. And furthermore, Christians are called to suffering in this life because of the torments of the devil, even more than others. Ultimately, all will be well when they enter immortality. Cyprian writes:

> It disturbs some that the power of this Disease attacks our people equally with the heathens, as if the Christian believed for this purpose, that he might have the enjoyment of the world and this life free from the contact of ills; and

not as one who undergoes all adverse things here and is reserved for future joy. It disturbs some that this mortality is common to us with others; and yet what is there in this world which is not common to us with others, so long as this flesh of ours still remains, according to the law of our first birth, common to us with them? So long as we are here in the world, we are associated with the human race in fleshly equality, but are separated in spirit. Therefore until this corruptible shall put on incorruption, and this mortal receive immortality, and the Spirit lead us to God the Father, whatsoever are the disadvantages of the flesh are common to us with the human race. Thus, when the earth is barren with an unproductive harvest, famine makes no distinction; thus, when with the invasion of the enemy any city is taken, captivity at once desolates all; and when serene clouds withhold the rain, the drought is alike to all; and when the jagged rocks rend the ship, the shipwreck is common without exception to all that sail in her; and the disease of the eyes, and the attack of fevers, and the feebleness of all the limbs is common to us with others, so long as this common flesh of ours is borne by us in the world. Moreover, if the Christian knows and keeps fast under what condition and what law he has believed, he will be aware that he must suffer more than others in the world, since he must struggle more with the attacks of the devil....

But perchance some one may object, and say, "It is this, then, that saddens me in the present mortality, that I, who had been prepared for confession, and had devoted myself to the endurance of suffering with my whole heart and with abundant courage, am deprived of martyrdom, in that I am anticipated by death." In the first place, martyrdom is not in your power, but in the condescension of God; neither can you say that you have lost what you do not know whether you would deserve to receive....

If we believe in Christ, let us have faith in His words and promises; and since we shall not die eternally, let us come with a glad security unto Christ, with whom we are both to conquer and to reign for ever. That in the meantime we die; we are passing over to immortality by death; nor can eternal life follow, unless it should befall us to depart from this life. That is not an ending, but a transit, and, this journey of time being traversed, a passage to eternity.[24]

Suffering is necessary for the Christian because the world is full of the temptations of the devil, which the Christian must work to combat. For Saint Cyprian, natural evil causes suffering for all human beings; with a poor harvest, all will go hungry. He also sees that suffering is particularly burdensome to Christians because they are engaged in a struggle with the devil, who has power over the world. Christians must take up the same battle that Jesus fought against evil, against the devil in this life. Saint Cyprian does recognize the glory of martyrdom and encourages his followers not to think too much of themselves and their spirituality in assuming that an early death from the plague would rob them of the honor of martyrdom; they may never have been worthy of that honor. He reminds them that their faith should save them from undue worry about dying, for true happiness can only be found in the life to come, in immortality: "Who would not crave to be changed and renewed into the likeness of Christ, and to arrive more quickly to the dignity of heavenly glory?"[25]

Saint Augustine, another church father, wrote a spiritual autobiography entitled *The Confessions*, published in A.D. 400, in which he said in prayer to God: "Thou hast formed us for Thyself, and our hearts are restless till they find rest in Thee."[26] He shares Cyprian's vision of the human destiny, as does C. S. Lewis, who writes:

The Christian doctrine of suffering explains, I believe, a very curious fact about the world we live in. The settled happiness and security which we all desire, God withholds from us by the very nature of the world: but joy, pleasure, merriment, He has scattered broadcast. We are never safe, but we have plenty of fun, and some ecstasy. It is not hard to see why. The security we crave would teach us to rest our hearts in this world and oppose an obstacle to our return to God: a few moments of happy love, a landscape, a symphony, a merry meeting with our friends, a bathe or a football match, have no such tendency. Our Father refreshes us on the journey with some pleasant inns, but will not encourage us to mistake them for home.[27]

Lewis would agree with the early fathers that ultimate happiness will not be achieved in this life; a certain loneliness and longing linger, an incompleteness and inadequacy, that beckon us to future fulfillment. Even at peace and happy, we are not satisfied.

In our quest to understand the meaning of suffering, we have looked at the heavy weight we bear in knowing of the evil in life. We have seen from C. S. Lewis's perspective that perhaps human courage and strength can develop despite great suffering, or because of it. Lewis suggests that suffering may be a message from God. Saint Cyprian considers suffering and death necessary for Christians to endure on their way to union with God in heaven. We also suffer because of love.

Unrequited love has been the force behind some of the greatest artistic expressions. It has created poetry, music, sculptures, plays, and paintings. Have you ever been swept away inside the rhythms and sounds of a piece of music that expresses what words cannot? The sounds of the Italian tenor Andrea Bocelli rise like incense, as he sings

For love,
have you ever spent everything, reason,
your pride, up to the tears?
You know tonight I remain.
I have no pretext,
only an obsession
that is still strong and mine
inside the soul you tear away.
And I tell you now,
sincere with myself,
how much it costs me to know you are
not mine,
and it would be as if
all this sea
drowned in me.[28]

The fulfillment of our desire for love has also brought expressions of ecstasy to life and literature. Human life is more than just the moment, the meal, the movie, the paycheck. There is an ethereal, timeless quality to human existence and desire. We suffer physical pain, emotional heartache, and mental anguish from evil, but also from love. The power of the human spirit to love is hard to describe, but it seems easy to give examples. Imagine the joy of a woman who has given birth to a child. She does not care how much pain was involved; in fact, the pain is quickly forgotten in the delight of the safe arrival of her baby. What of the anonymous man who dove into the icy waters of the Potomac River in Washington, D.C., to rescue some of the passengers of a jet that had crashed—and then got into his car and went home? What about fire fighters who enter burning buildings, risking their lives to save the lives of perfect strangers? Our ability and desire to love leads us into suffering, willingly or unwillingly.

At the age of fifty-four, C. S. Lewis was settled in the comfortable life of an Oxford don. He had achieved an international following as a writer of children's books and of Christian spirituality. He was lost in his scholarly world, surrounded by history and orderliness, by his friends and bachelor ways. Joy Davidman Greshem traveled from the United States to meet him in September 1952.[29] Their friendship grew in the ensuing years. When Joy needed to secure British citizenship to stay in England, Lewis agreed to marry her, in name only. In October 1956 Joy was diagnosed with bone cancer, and Lewis began a journey of love and faithfulness that endured beyond the grave. They married in spirit and in flesh, in the presence of a priest, on March 27, 1957. Lewis wrote of these events to a friend, Dorothy Sayers, on June 25, 1957,

> I ought to tell you my own news. On examination it turned out that Joy's previous marriage, made in her pre-Christian days, was no marriage: the man had a wife still living. The Bishop of Oxford said it was not the present policy to approve re-marriage in such cases....Then dear Father Bide (do you know him?) who had come to lay his hands on Joy—for he has on his record what looks v. like one miracle—without being asked and merely on being told the situation at once said he wd. marry us. So we had a bedside marriage with a nuptial Mass. When I last wrote to you I could not even have wished this: you will gather (and may say "guessed as much") that my feelings had changed. They say a rival often turns a friend into a lover. Thanatos, certainly (they say) approaching but at an uncertain speed, is a most efficient rival for this purpose. We soon learn to love what we know we must love....My heart is breaking and I was never so happy before; at any rate there is more in life than I knew about.[30]

A moment of time is created for them. Joy experiences a remission in the cancer; Lewis endures tremendous physical pain. He believes that God has given him Joy's pain so that she may experience relief. The doctors think Joy's remission is a miracle. Neville Coghill had lunch with Lewis and recalled this conversation:

> Shortly after Lewis' marriage, when he brought his wife to lunch with me, he said to me, looking at her across the grassy quadrangle, "I never expected to have, in my sixties, the happiness that passed me by in my twenties." It was then that he told me of having been allowed to accept her pain.
>
> "You mean" (I said) "that the pain left her, and that you felt it for her in your body?"
>
> "Yes," he said, "in my legs. It was crippling. But it relieved hers."[31]

The remission ends in October 1959. They take a last vacation together with friends to Greece in April 1960, and she dies swiftly on July 13, 1960. Lewis writes of his anguish after her death in *A Grief Observed*, a collection of thoughts that he had been keeping in small notebooks, a diary of his suffering:

> No one ever told me that grief felt so like fear. I am not afraid, but the sensation is like being afraid. The same fluttering in the stomach, the same restlessness, the yawning. I keep on swallowing.
>
> At other times it feels like being mildly drunk, or concussed. There is a sort of invisible blanket between the world and me. I find it hard to take in what anyone says. Or perhaps, hard to want to take it in. It is so uninteresting. Yet I want the others to be about me. I dread the moments when the house is empty. If only they would talk to one another and not to me.[32]

It seems that Lewis thought life was full of small contentments that would never distract him from the life ahead. The shock of falling so deeply in love and enduring the pain of separation from his beloved gave him an unexpected challenge. He questions the meaning of suffering, railing against God: "My real fear is...that we are really rats in a trap. Or worse still, rats in a laboratory....Supposing the truth were 'God always vivisects?'"[33] He cannot understand why Joy had to suffer so much pain or why they are now separated by the veil of death. His pain must be shared by Joy, even on the other side of death, he thinks; how can one lover be happy, while the other grieves? He remembers the fierceness with which she vowed that she would come for him on his deathbed.

> If, as I can't help suspecting, the dead also feel the pains of separation (and this may be one of their purgatorial sufferings), then for both lovers, and for all pairs of lovers without exception, bereavement is a universal and integral part of our experience of love. It follows marriage as normally as marriage follows courtship or as autumn follows summer.[34]

Their love story inspired William Nicholson to write the screenplay *Shadowlands*, which won the 1990 London *Evening Standard* Best Play Award. It was later made into a movie by Richard Attenborough. The play ends with Lewis in a familiar moment, speaking before a large audience about his understanding of the "problem of pain." Only now, his words reflect a depth of understanding, and a lack of understanding, that dig in deeper than Lewis at forty-six could have foreseen:

> We are like blocks of stone, out of which the sculptor carves the forms of men. The blows of his chisel, which hurt us so much, are what make us perfect. No shadows

here. Only darkness, and silence, and the pain that cries like a child.

It ends, like all affairs of the heart, with exhaustion. Only so much pain is possible. Then, rest.

So it comes about that, when I am quiet, when I am quiet, she returns to me. There she is, in my mind, in my memory, coming towards me, and I love her again as I did before, even though I know I will lose her again, and be hurt again.

So you can say if you like that Jack Lewis has no answer to the question after all, except this: I have been given the choice twice in my life. The boy chose safety. The man chooses suffering. (He now speaks to her, in his memory.)

I went to my wardrobe this morning. I was looking for my old brown jacket, the one I used to wear before—I'd forgotten that you'd carried out one of your purges there. Just before we went to Greece, I think it was.

I find I can live with the pain, after all. The pain, now, is part of the happiness, then. That's the deal.

Only shadows, Joy.[35]

Nicholson gets into the skin of Lewis, mining his writings, probing his friends, and touching the truth of his experience of love and loss because, as a human being, Nicholson will follow the same path and find the same walls and bridges. It is not only Lewis's story, it is ours.

Conclusion

When she was nine years old, my daughter Kathryn said to me, "If there really are people on Mars, I hope they find out after I am dead." I laugh as I remember it, but I think I can understand her. She was saying that there is only so much she can take of change, raw, earth-shaking, world-shattering change, and then she just can't cope. Much of what we have discussed in this chapter borders on the "just can't cope." Life itself is a mystery, and so is death. We looked at myths that shaped a cosmos, and a story of life on earth. The Book of Genesis does its best to situate humanity in a universe that God has created, where order reigns, and life has purpose. It identifies the bitter reality of human suffering and death, explaining that we are at the root of it. Scientists have taught us much about the workings of the universe, but they have not solved the mystery of why. The Christian myth of Jesus' birth responds both to the mystery of life and human destiny and to the problem of evil. There is no doubt that human beings have "a problem" with evil.

Our discussion of suffering began with setting terms and parameters: physical pain and psychological suffering, moral evil (both personal and social), and natural evil. We examined both Jewish and Christian spirituality in the face of suffering and historical writings from the traditions and twentieth-century writers. The authors recognized both the power of evil and the resilience of the human spirit. But human instinct and wisdom do not give us certainties. They are beliefs. And the questions really are only beginning. We have yet to address a critical issue: Where is God in human suffering?

2

Suffering

Vanity of vanities, says Qoheleth, / vanity of vanities! All things are vanity!...

I saw wicked men approach and enter; and as they left the sacred place, they were praised in the city for what they had done. This also is vanity. Because the sentence against evildoers is not promptly executed, therefore the hearts of men are filled with the desire to commit evil—because the sinner does evil a hundred times and survives. Though indeed I know that it shall be well with those who fear God, for their reverence toward him; and that it shall not be well with the wicked man, and he shall not prolong his shadowy days, for his lack of reverence toward God.

This is a vanity which occurs on earth: there are just men treated as though they had done evil and wicked men treated as though they had done justly....

When I applied my heart to know wisdom and to observe what is done on earth, I recognized that man is unable to find out all God's work that is done under the sun, even though neither by day nor by night do his eyes find rest in sleep. However much man toils in searching, he does not find it out; and even if the wise man says that he knows, he is unable to find it out. (Eccl 1:2; 8:10–14, 16–17)

The wisdom of Qoheleth, a teacher who lived around 300 B.C., is that he sees the stark reality of life. He sees death as the horizon for every human being and the "vanity" of achievements, possessions, and ambition, for "as he came forth from his mother's womb, so again shall he depart, naked as he came, having nothing from his labor that he can carry in his hand" (Eccl 5:14). Besides the wall of death that awaits, Qoheleth considers other issues, one of which is the fact that the wicked seem to prosper, seem to enjoy the fruits of their ill-gotten gains without punishment. Qoheleth still has faith that "it shall be well with those who fear God," but he does not believe that human beings really understand the ways of God.

In this chapter we consider the question of judgement. Why does God permit evil? We must consider the nature of human life, the existence of suffering and apparent injustice, and wonder about the goodness of God and the issue of accountability. Is there order in the universe, and if so, who is responsible for the chaos that threatens it? Are human beings held responsible for their actions, either in the present life or in some future existence?

Why Does God Permit Evil?

The word is *theodicy*, theological explanations that attempt to reconcile what is apparently impossible to reconcile: a perfectly good and all-powerful God who permits evil.[1] Christian tradition holds that God is love, an all-powerful creator who made the world, which was "good." God created human beings for happiness. And yet, there is great misery, and life ends in death. Why would a loving God permit human beings to suffer and die? Either God is not good, and did not intend humanity for happiness, or God is not powerful enough to conquer evil, that is, God is not God. Six philosophers of religion from the Claremont Colleges constructed a complex set of arguments on the topic in the book entitled *Encountering Evil*. They present the following options:

1. God does not exist.
2. God is not responsible for evil, human beings are.

3. God allows evil so that human beings can grow.

4. God must be challenged, God-against-God, in protest.

We will examine these options in the hope that they will shed some light on the problem.

God does not exist. The twentieth century saw the rise of atheism as both a philosophical and a societal reality. Many who argue against the existence of God base their position on the overwhelming reality of evil. Stephen Davis, John Cobb, David Griffin, John Hick, John Roth, and Frederick Sontag, the contributors to *Encountering Evil,* acknowledge philosophers like David Hume, social revolutionaries like Karl Marx, and others who take this stance. But they choose not to do so. They struggle to find another way.

God is not responsible for evil, human beings are. This theodicy has two components: God created human beings with free will; they are independent in thought and deed, capable of writing their own futures. With their freedom, as evidenced by the story of the fall, human beings grasped at power and control, thus bringing evil into the world. Human beings continue to sin, continue to choose against the goodness of God's design. God does not create the evil that exists. Stephen Davis presents this argument, attributing the authorship of the free-will defense to Saint Augustine.[2] Saint Augustine wrote "On Free Will" between 388 and 395, "The Enchiridion on Faith, Hope, and Love," in 421, and "On Grace and Free Will" in 427. In "The Enchiridion," he summarizes his views on free will:

> As it is right that we should know the causes of good and evil, so much of them at least as will suffice for the way that leads us to the kingdom, where there will be life without the shadow of death, truth without any allow of error, and happiness unbroken by any sorrow....I think there cannot now be any doubt, that the only cause of any good that we

enjoy is the goodness of God, and that the only cause of evil is the falling away from the unchangeable good of a being made good but changeable, first in the case of an angel, and afterwards in the case of man....

And so it happens that all descended from [Adam], and from the woman who had led him into sin, and was condemned with him—were tainted with the original sin, and were drawn through divers errors and sufferings into that last and endless punishment which they suffer in common with the fallen angels, their corrupters and masters, and the partakers of their doom....

Thus, then, matters stood. The whole mass of the human race was under condemnation, was lying steeped and wallowing in misery, and was being tossed from one form of evil to another, and, having joined the faction of the fallen angels, was paying the well-merited penalty of that impious rebellion. For whatever the wicked freely do through blind and unbridled lust, and whatever they suffer against their will in the way of open punishment, this all evidently pertains to the just wrath of God. But the goodness of the Creator never fails either to supply life and vital power to the wicked angels (without their existence would soon come to an end); or, in the case of mankind, who spring from a condemned and corrupt stock, to impart form and life to their seed, to fashion their members, and through the various seasons of their life, and in the different parts of the earth, to quicken their senses, and bestow upon them the nourishment they need. For He judged it better to bring good out of evil, than not to permit any evil to exist.[3]

Saint Augustine accepted the events recorded in the Genesis account of the fall as fact. To his mind, Adam and Eve were directly and concretely responsible for the first sin because they were not faithful to God. That original sin "taints" their descendants. Augustine marvels at the mercy of God, who continued to "supply life and vital power" to the wicked, both angels and human beings, and who will allow for a "restoration of happiness" for the human race.[4]

In "On Grace and Free Will" Augustine writes "now He has revealed to us, through His Holy Scriptures, that there is in a man a free choice of will."[5] One of the texts he cites in chapter 3 is from the letter of James. Some scholars suggest that this is James "the brother of the Lord," who was the leader of the Jewish Christian community of Jerusalem, and they consider the letter as one of the earliest of the New Testament:[6]

> Blessed is the man who perseveres in temptation, for when he has been proved he will receive the crown of life that he promised to those who love him. No one experiencing temptation should say, "I am being tempted by God"; for God is not subject to temptation to evil, and he himself tempts no one. Rather, each person is tempted when he is lured and enticed by his own desire. Then desire conceives and brings forth sin, and when sin reaches maturity it gives birth to death. (Jas 1:12–15)

For Augustine, the origin of evil is in the human heart, where unbridled desire and ambition betray the soul and distract us from the goodness we should seek.

For Stephen Davis, who defines himself as "an analytic philosopher and an evangelical Christian," the free-will defense seems rational and conforms to the depths of his religious convictions about life, scripture, and the nature of God. He writes, "I believe that all truth is from God and is consistent with the existence, goodness, and omnipotence of God."[7] For Davis, responsibility for moral evil falls on human beings. At creation God gave human beings freedom, the right to create their own lives and determine their own fate. The weakness, selfishness, greed, and stupidity of human beings create suffering and pain for others. This tragic reality needs the healing presence of the incarnate Christ. Davis sees human sinfulness as responsible for moral evil but recognizes that this way of thinking leaves natural evil unexplained.

Over the years Davis has come to agree with Alvin Plantinga, who writes on this question in *God, Freedom, and Evil*. Davis comments:

> In recent years Alvin Plantinga has suggested that the FWD [free-will defense] can indeed solve the problem of natural evil. He appeals to an often neglected aspect of Christian tradition, which was also used by Augustine in his writings on the problem of evil, viz, the notion of Satan or Lucifer as the cause of natural evil. Augustine, Plantinga says, "attributes much of the evil we find to Satan or to Satan and his cohorts. Satan, so the traditional doctrine goes, is a mighty nonhuman spirit who, along with many other angels, was created long before God created man. Unlike most of his colleagues, Satan rebelled against God and has been wreaking whatever havoc he can. The result is natural evil. So the natural evil we find is due to the free actions of nonhuman spirits."[8]

Responsibility for natural evil lies with other "nonhuman spirits" who seek destruction and chaos for humanity. Davis readily admits, however, as did Plantinga, that because many today do not accept the existence of any sort of devil or demon, this explanation may land with a dull thud. Nonetheless, Davis finds this explanation logically complementary to the free-will defense and, for himself, intellectually and religiously satisfactory.

Thus Davis presents the classic approach of Augustine on the question of evil: God permits evil, because God gave human beings free will. Human beings use that freedom for good and for ill, and God allows human history to unfold accordingly. Davis raises a new question for us: Who or what is the devil? Does the devil exist? And if so, what affect does this rebellious spirit have on human life? These questions will be addressed more comprehensively in the next chapter. Nonetheless, it is worthwhile to note here the pervasive presence of the devil in popular religious belief, from primitive roots in Egypt, Babylon, and Persia,[9] to modern-day recognition—a poll taken in 1997 showed that 63 percent of the people surveyed believe in hell.[10] The psychologist Carl Jung recognized the devil as "the shadow," one of the archetypes of the collective unconscious.[11] The impulse to find an embodiment of evil in the world is an ancient and pervasive practice.

God allows evil so that human beings can grow. John Hick builds this argument on the writings of Saint Irenaeus, bishop of Lyons, who lived from A.D. 120 to 202. Hick comments that Irenaeus's insight was not systematically developed in the way that Augustine's treatises on free will were.[12] In considering the narratives of Genesis, the story of creation and the fall of Adam and Eve, Irenaeus wrote that we are made in God's image, but we must grow to God's likeness. This is the natural destiny of humanity, and Irenaeus did not consider the sin of Adam and Eve to completely devastate this original destiny.[13] Irenaeus writes:

> Man being originated and formed comes to be in the image and likeness of the Unoriginate God: The Father approving and commanding, The Son performing and creating, The Spirit giving nourishment and growth, and Man for his part silently advancing, and going onward to perfection; i.e., coming near the Unoriginate. For the Unoriginate is perfect; and this is God. And it was needful that Man should first be brought into being, and being made should grow, and having grown should come to Manhood, and after

Manhood should be multiplied, and being multiplied should grow in strength, and after such growth should be glorified, and being gloried should see his own Lord.[14]

Hick develops his theory of morality based on this perspective. For him, image and likeness become two stages in the process of human development:

Thus existence "in the image of God" was a potentiality for knowledge of and relationship with one's Maker rather than such knowledge and relationship as a fully realized state. In other words, people were created as spiritually and morally immature creatures, at the beginning of a long process of further growth and development, which constitutes the second stage of God's creative work. In this second stage, of which we are a part, the intelligent, ethical, and religious animal is being brought through one's own free responses into what Irenaeus called the divine "likeness." The human animal is being created into a child of God.[15]

This process can be understood to conform to certain principles. The first Hick terms "epistemic distance." A finite creature would have no life, no freedom, in relation to the infinite God, "the limitless divine reality and power, goodness and love, knowledge and wisdom, towering above one's self."[16] To allow for human development, God must stand at a distance, giving human beings full reign and control over this world. Hick believes that this would ultimately provide the opportunity for humanity to grow freely into a relationship with God.

The second principle Hick proposes is that human beings do not grow into goodness in a "static environment."[17] "In a world devoid both of dangers to be avoided and rewards to be won," he writes, "we may assume that there would have been virtually no development of the human intellect and imagination."[18] It is the bitter struggles for life, the wrestling with one's soul, the hard climb toward moral perfection through adversity and challenge, that create truly moral beings. This is the story of the human race, and it is the saga of every person.

In conclusion, Hick sees this process of divinization as necessarily incomplete in a lifetime. His theory of ultimate reconciliation of God and humanity, of the perfection and happiness of the human race, needs eternity.

> It is very evident that this person-making process, leading eventually to perfect human community, is not completed on this earth. It is not completed in the life of the individual—or at best only in the few who have attained to sanctification, or moksha, or nirvana on this earth. Clearly the enormous majority of men and women die without having attained to this....And it is equally evident that the perfect all-embracing human community, in which self-regarding concern has been transcended in mutual love, not only has not been realized in this world, but never can be, since hundreds of generations of human beings have already lived and died.[19]

Why does God permit evil? According to an Irenaean theodicy, God permits evil in order to allow human beings the greatest freedom and control over their own lives. The permanent inequality between the infinite creator and the finite creature could have been overbearing and oppressive. Humanity would have been dwarfed and may never have achieved any greatness in the face of such an overpowering force. As it is, suggests Hick, God is a quiet presence in a world that is the full responsibility of human beings. If over the course of human development, there are human beings drawn to a relationship with their creator, then they seek that relationship by choice. To be made in

God's image is to be made with a spark of divinity, which opens up a future that is not bound by space and time. To grow in God's likeness is to achieve moral perfection, to become a part of the life and love that energize the universe. For finite creatures the path to moral perfection is arduous. On their way to a perfect community, societies have failed miserably, with hatred, prejudice, and self-interest dominating the course of history. And yet, the rise of democracy, the end of racially segregated South Africa, and the tearing down of the Berlin Wall are quiet signs that human history is changing, that ideals command their own attention. Hick sees this process as coming to full fruition beyond ordinary space and time. For justice and happiness to be complete, they must be shared by all human beings, not just the last society on earth after millennia of struggle. Therefore, full fruition depends on the ultimate reconciliation and union with God after this life for every human person.[20]

Not everything has been said on the question of evil, however. As Stephen Davis points out, "One of the obvious weaknesses of many theodicies is that they cannot account for the huge amount of evil that apparently exists in the world."[21] There remain the deaths of six million Jews in concentration camps during World War II, the atrocities of war in Bosnia-Herzogovinia, the starvation of peoples in Ethiopia—events of the twentieth century alone. Human history is fraught with outrageous acts of brutality and hatred. What can be said of God and evil in the face of the raw fact of human violence? For some, the answer becomes a protest.

God must be challenged, God-against-God, in protest. John Roth, a professor of philosophy, argues for just this position.[22] There is simply too much human destruction for us to feel comfortable with traditional explanations and beliefs about God and human moral responsibility. Roth sees individuals who have been victimized by human violence speaking out in protest, challenging a God who would allow such brutality. In particular, he quotes the writings of Elie Wiesel, one of the great spiritual leaders of the Jewish community rising from the ashes of World War II: "If I am given the choice of feeling sorry for Him or for human beings, I choose the latter anytime. He is big enough, strong enough to take care of Himself; man is not."[23] A theodicy of protest, according to Roth, is determined by a stance that challenges the state of the world.

> Imperfect as it is, the theodicy explored here does origi-
> nate in felt needs. Two are fundamental: a sense that
> human affairs are far worse than any good reason can jus-
> tify or than our powers alone can alter; and, second, a
> yearning that refuses to settle for despair that the first feel-
> ing generates.[24]

For Roth, human misery cannot be explained away by plac-ing responsibility on human shoulders. Ultimately, the evil expe-rienced far overshadows any potential for human moral development. The end does not justify the means. Whatever goal God had in mind in permitting evil has been completely obliter-ated by what history has wrought. Roth considers the current state of affairs irretrievably damaged and beyond human ability to correct. It would take the work of a divine being to transform human misery into happiness, and that divine being refuses to act. And so Roth and others stand "in protest," calling upon the God of life and love to challenge the God in power. According to Roth a theodicy of protest does not draw one into despair; it is a fight against hopelessness. It is holding up the purity of real goodness as the ideal and challenging all comers, including God, to live up to it. In this way Roth finds a way to continue to believe in something.

When challenged by colleagues to explain the basis of his hope, Roth responds:

In the words of the Christian creed from Nicaea, I "look for the resurrection of the dead, and the life of the world to come." Thus, I hope that Jankiel Wiernik [a Holocaust survivor] will laugh again—joyously, honestly, without his past paled into insignificance, and without derangement. As for life right now, I hope that waste, such as that which stole Wiernik's laughter, can be checked. In this world I expect no ultimate beating of swords into plowshares, but absence of strenuous effort in that direction will be more than a sin. It will move toward punishment itself, for indifference to our own existence may finish us all. If that realization does not foster protesting hope against despair, we are in deep trouble.[25]

Roth holds onto his faith in hope itself.

In exploring the question of why God permits evil, we have found different paths to choose. We have seen that God has given human beings freedom, which may very well have led to the overpowering reality of evil in the world. Human beings may be the cause of great failure and misery. There may have been a reason to permit some evil, to allow human beings to explore and develop in complete autonomy so as to earn their right to eternity. Others argue that even these possible explanations pale in the face of the magnitude of human suffering. They question whether we can really accept the goodness of God. David Griffin suggests that God's power is persuasive rather than coercive.[26] Perhaps, Griffin argues, God is doing what is possible to influence humanity.

> Some theologians might agree that we have power, even power in relation to God, and yet say that God could overpower us and hence totally determine our activities, including our willing and desiring. But that is excluded by what I mean by saying that we have inherent in relation to God.

The claim is precisely that our self-determining activity, and the consequent influence we have on others, cannot be totally controlled by God. Hence God cannot control but only persuade what we become and how we affect others.[27]

The marionette strings are missing. God cannot reign in human freedom at will, when things get out of hand. Rather, according to Griffin, humanity has real power that even God cannot undo. And so, moving full circle, we see the possibility that there might be a limit to God's goodness (according to Roth) or to God's power (according to Griffin). Although we have explored the various paths, the answer is illusive. The six philosophers struggle to hold onto their sense of hope in the face of evil. For the Christian community, inspired by its Judaic heritage, the question of where God is in the midst of human suffering is answered by a symbol: the cross. The next question: Where is God while human beings suffer?

Where Is God While Human Beings Suffer?

But the third rope was still moving; being so light, the child was still alive....For more than a half an hour he stayed there, struggling between life and death, dying in slow agony under our eyes....

Behind me I heard [a] man asking: "Where is God now?" And I heard a voice within me answer him: "Where is He? Here He is—He is hanging here on this gallows."[28]

Elie Wiesel, of whom much has been said in this text, concluded his reflections on the hanging of this child at Auschwitz by stating that he knew where God was. God was hanging on that rope. That God stands with the innocent who are suffering is a basic belief of the people of Israel. God is Shekinah, the indwelling spirit who joins the people in their exile, in their struggles, in their suffering. Also, in the writings of the prophet Isaiah, there are recorded four Songs of the Suffering Servant. They describe "the sinless Servant, who by his voluntary suffering atones for the sins of his people, and saves them from just punishment at the hands of God."[29] The Suffering Servant is a mysterious figure who takes on the suffering not only of the innocent but even of those who have sinned against God.

> If he gives his life as an offering for sin,
>> he shall see his descendants in a long life,
>> and the will of the LORD shall be accomplished through him.
> Because of his affliction
>> he shall see the light in fullness of days;
> Through his suffering, my servant shall justify many,
>> and their guilt he shall bear.
> Therefore I will give him his portion among the great,
>> and he shall divide the spoils with the mighty,
> Because he surrendered himself to death
>> and was counted among the wicked;
> And he shall take away the sins of many,
>> and win pardon for their offenses. (Isa 53:10b–12)

The Spirit of God, Shekinah, and the Suffering Servant are two examples of Old Testament belief in the presence of God in the midst of suffering. God is not distant but present. Elie Wiesel's observation that God was hanging on the rope represents a depth of understanding and spiritual trust in God that continues to express this tradition. It is its own kind of protest: God is not the cause of evil. Even just punishment is alleviated by God.

When his son Aaron was diagnosed with a congenital illness that would eventually lead to his premature death at fourteen years of age, Rabbi Harold Kushner had to make sense of his own life, and the life of his son, as much as he had to take care of the members of his congregation and all of their heartaches and struggles. From the depth of his spirituality and his religious tradition, Rabbi Kushner comes to peace with life, with death, and with God. He writes:

> God does not cause our misfortunes. Some are caused by bad luck, some are caused by bad people, and some are simply an inevitable consequence of our being human and being mortal, living in a world of inflexible natural laws. The painful things that happen to us are not punishments for our misbehavior, nor are they in any way part of some grand design on God's part. Because the tragedy is not God's will, we need not feel hurt or betrayed by God when tragedy strikes. We can turn to Him for help in overcoming it, precisely because we can tell ourselves that God is as outraged by it as we are.[30]

"Because the tragedy is not God's will," Rabbi Kushner writes, God stands with us in adversity. God's response is the same as ours: outrage. Kushner acknowledges the Christian perspective of a God "who suffers" and says that although he does not understand exactly what that might mean, he believes that God is "the source of my being able to feel sympathy and outrage, and that He is on the same side when we stand with the victim against those who would hurt him."[31] Kushner sees that the workings of the universe create the structures that make life possible. It does not make sense to him that God would interfere with natural law; what kind of life would we have if God would stop gravity for one person, or have another survive a fire without being burned? Chaos would replace order, and no one could function. Even pain serves a purpose. It serves as the body's alert system, a warning that there is possible injury or illness.[32] Kushner does not accept misfortune as punishment from God for sin. Temporal retribution—that is, the good are rewarded in this life with happiness and the sinful are punished by failure and loss—is a belief inherent in Judaic spirituality, but it is one that Kushner rejects. For him, heartbreak and disappointments find their way into human life in ways that can be understood from within the natural order.

Even the perverse destructiveness of the Holocaust does not change Kushner's faith in God. He quotes a Holocaust survivor who feels the same way:

> It never occurred to me to question God's doings or lack of doings while I was an inmate of Auschwitz, although of course I understand others did....I was no less or no more religious because of what the Nazis did to us; and I believe my faith in God was not undermined in the least. It never occurred to me to associate the calamity we were experiencing with God, to blame Him, or to believe in Him less or cease believing in Him at all because He didn't come to our aid. God doesn't owe us that, or anything. We owe our lives to Him. If someone believes God is responsible for the death of six million because He didn't somehow do something to save them, he's got his thinking reversed. We owe God our lives for the few or many years we live, and we have the duty to worship Him and do as He commands us. That's what we're here on earth for, to be in God's service, to do God's bidding.[33]

The Book of Job, a classic meditation on suffering, raises a question about the love of God. As the Latin American theologian Gustavo Gutiérrez states it: "Can human beings have a disinterested faith in God—that is, can they believe in God without looking for rewards and fearing punishments? Even more specifically: Are human beings capable, in the midst of unjust suffering, of continuing to assert their faith in God and speak of God without expecting a return?"[34] We will revisit this question in the next chapter. But here we can note that within the spirituality of the

Old Testament, expressed above by a Holocaust survivor, is the expectation that human beings will honor the one who created them and gave them life. That devotion is not conditional.

The indwelling Spirit of God is with the people, especially when they are in trouble. This Old Testament assumption of the presence of God, who hears the cry of the people, reflects a God who saves.

> When the Egyptians maltreated and oppressed us, impos-
> ing hard labor upon us, we cried to the LORD, the God of
> our fathers, and he heard our cry and saw our affliction,
> our toil and our oppression. He brought us out of Egypt
> with his strong hand and outstretched arm, with terrifying
> power, with signs and wonders; and bringing us into this
> country, he gave us this land flowing with milk and honey.
> (Deut 26:6–9)

That is the essence of the Exodus narrative, that through Moses God led the people out of slavery in Egypt and brought them to the Promised Land. The Suffering Servant of Isaiah shows the ability of one person to embody the community and heal its wounds, conquer its sinfulness. This Suffering Servant became a way for the followers of Jesus Christ to understand his life, death, and resurrection. The crucifixion is both symbol and reality in the history of Christianity. The people of Israel were waiting for a messiah, one who would save them from their oppressors, the Romans. Jesus was to become the Suffering Servant, the Messiah, although the way in which he took on these roles generated an explosion of fury and change in the life of the people of Israel, and indeed the life of the Western world.

John the Baptist brought Jesus' public ministry into focus when he baptized him in the Jordan River. Following the narrative in the Gospel of Mark, John draws people to consider their sins and hope for the coming of the one who will "baptize you with the Holy Spirit." (Mark 1:8) Jesus was identified to the people at the moment of his baptism when "a voice came from the heavens, [saying] 'You are my beloved Son; with you I am well pleased'" (Mark 1:11). Jesus began a life of preaching and healing as he traveled around Galilee. He called disciples to him, ordinary people, fishermen. As he entered towns, people brought the sick to him for healing. Jesus preached to them, telling them parables about the coming of the kingdom of God. Crowds gathered to hear him. Yet when he entered the synagogue in Nazareth, where he had grown up, "they took offense at him" (Mark 6:3), and he could do nothing there. Nonetheless, he sent his own followers out to continue his work: "They went off and preached repentance. They drove out many demons, and they anointed with oil many who were sick and cured them" (Mark 6:12–13). In the meantime, John the Baptist had been killed by King Herod because he had challenged the propriety of Herod's marriage.

Mark keeps his story very simple. The Gospels of Matthew, Luke, and John contain prayers and sermons by Jesus, as well as long discussions of how Jesus understands God. Mark is interested in connecting his story of Jesus to the Songs of the Suffering Servant in order to draw people to believe that Jesus is the Messiah, the one who is to come to save the people of Israel. And so Jesus "began to teach them that the Son of Man must suffer greatly and be rejected by the elders, the chief priests, and the scribes, and be killed, and rise after three days" (Mark 8:31). His own followers, Peter especially, could not understand or accept what Jesus predicted. But Jesus is adamant: "Whoever wishes to come after me must deny himself, take up his cross, and follow me" (Mark 8:34). Peter, James, and John experience the transfiguration, the transformation of Jesus as he is united with Elijah and Moses. James and John vie for a position of honor in the kingdom to come, but Jesus warns them of the suffering that will involve. Rather than seek honor or power, they must become servants.

Jesus' entrance into Jerusalem just before Passover, the celebration of the Exodus from Egypt, rallies the people, and they proclaim "Hosanna! / Blessed is he who comes in the name of the Lord!" (Mark 11:9). He chases away the moneychangers from the Temple, attracting the attention of the chief priests and scribes who were then resolved to have him put to death. His preaching becomes more strident as he challenges the practices of the scribes. Jesus gathers his disciples together to celebrate the Passover meal, and as they eat and drink together, he stands and offers the prayers. Only he doesn't quite *say* them. Instead,

> he took bread, said the blessing, broke it, and gave it to them and said, "Take it; this is my body." Then he took a cup, gave thanks, and gave it to them, and they all drank from it. He said to them, "This is my blood of the covenant, which will be shed for many. Amen, I say to you, I shall not drink again the fruit of the vine until the day when I drink it new in the kingdom of God." (Mark 14:22–25)

Events transpire quickly now. Jesus and his followers go to the Garden of Gethsemane, outside the walls of Jerusalem. They are followed there, and Jesus is arrested. He is accused before the Sanhedrin, the governing body of Israel, of blasphemy and condemned. In the morning he is taken to Pilate, the Roman procurator. Pilate questions him and offers to release him. But the chief priests incite the crowd, which shouts to have him crucified. Pilate acquiesces, and Jesus is taken off by Roman soldiers, who beat him and drag him out of the city to crucify him. Jesus staggers along the way, and Simon is pulled from the crowd to help him carry his cross. Jesus is nailed to a cross between two revolutionaries.

At noon darkness came over the whole land until three in the afternoon. And at three o'clock Jesus cried out in a loud voice, *"Eloi, Eloi, lema sabachthani?"* which is translated, "My God, my God, why have you forsaken me?" Some of the bystanders who heard it said, "Look, he is calling Elijah." One of them ran, soaked a sponge with wine, put it on a reed, and gave it to him to drink, saying, "Wait, let us see if Elijah comes to take him down." Jesus gave a loud cry and breathed his last. (Mark 15:33–37)

Jesus' body is taken down and buried in a stone tomb. Mary Magdalene and Mary the mother of Joses follow to see where he is buried. After the sabbath, Mary Magdalene, Mary, the mother of James, and Salome return to the tomb, prepared to anoint Jesus' body. What they discover astonishes them. The stone covering the entrance to the tomb has been rolled away, and in the place of the body there sits a young man. He says to them,

> "Do not be amazed! You seek Jesus of Nazareth, the crucified. He has been raised; he is not here. Behold, the place where they laid him. But go and tell his disciples and Peter, 'He is going before you to Galilee; there you will see him, as he told you.'" (Mark 16:6–7)

Thus the Gospel of Mark concludes, announcing that the one who has been crucified has been raised from the dead. Resurrection accounts follow, in Mark and the other gospels, in which Jesus appears to the disciples, eats with them, comforts them, and inspires them to continue his work.

> The eleven disciples went to Galilee, to the mountain to which Jesus had ordered them. When they saw them, they worshiped, but they doubted. Then Jesus approached and said to them, "All power in heaven and on earth has been

given to me. Go, therefore, and make disciples of all nations, baptizing them in the name of the Father, and of the Son, and of the Holy Spirit, teaching them to observe all that I have commanded you. And behold, I am with you always, until the end of the age." (Matt 28:16–20)

Many questions remain. Can we make sense out of a claim that the divine creator took on a human existence? How is that possible? Even if it is possible, why would it happen? Given the simple narrative in the Gospel of Mark, what did Jesus actually do to deserve such a brutal death? What difference does it make to the course of human history that this man Jesus lived and died and appeared again to his friends and followers after his death? As to the how and why of incarnation, these questions have been the meat of theological reflection throughout the history of Christianity. *Kenosis* is the theological term used to describe God's capacity to become "less than" the infinite perfection of divinity. The possibility of the incarnation rests on God's action of "self-emptying." The traditional argument in favor of this potentiality states that God's perfect nature would be "less than perfect" if there were any limits to God's ability. Not to be able to become human would be a limitation. Therefore, the possibility of God's self-emptying action to become human must exist.

Karl Rahner, a Catholic priest and theologian, had evolution in mind when he presented his understanding of the incarnation, which he builds upon his view that "it is of the intrinsic nature of matter to develop towards spirit."[35] Rahner sees the transformation of matter into spirit as the key to understanding both the possibility and the fundamental nature of the hypostatic union, "the permanent union of a human nature with the divine Person of the Logos."[36]

If we take as our starting point the unity of spirit and matter, and this does not mean homogeneity, then we have to try to understand man as the existent in whom the basic tendency of matter to discover itself in spirit through self-transcendence reaches its definitive breakthrough, so that from this perspective the essence of man himself can be seen within a fundamental and total conception of the world. But it is this very essence of man which, through its free and highest and full self-transcendence gratuitously made possible for him by God, it is this essence which is "awaiting" its fulfillment and that of the world in what we call in Christian concepts grace and glory.

The permanent beginning and the absolute guarantee that this ultimate self-transcendence, which is fundamentally unsurpassable, will succeed and has already begun is what we call the "hypostatic union."[37]

From Rahner's perspective, Jesus Christ is the most complete example of the fundamental reality of evolution, that of matter transforming into spirit, nonlife into life. The moment when creation changed from matter into living matter is a provocative one: How did this impossibility become a reality? The scientists don't know why, they just know that it did. For Rahner, this union of matter and spirit, begun in primitive ways, was destined to one day achieve perfection. The perfect union of matter and spirit occurred in Jesus whose life became the ultimate moment when earth and divinity unite (for what is life if not participation in the divine reality?). The human capacity for self-transcendence, for participation in spirit existing in a complex way not entirely bound by space and time, is itself a gift from God.

These comments on the incarnation provide a few insights into what it might mean in Christian belief to talk about God fully present in human existence, not only as Shekinah but uniquely as a human being. Our other question, why was Jesus put to death, can be answered by looking at his life, what he did, where he went, what he said and how it affected people.

Another twentieth-century theologian, <u>Thomas Hart</u>, sees the essence of Jesus in this way:

> He lives for God. He is totally centered in God. The God of Jesus is gentle, nurturing, faithful, tender, creative, compassionate. He trusts God, even when trust is hardest. He sees God's creative hand and providence everywhere. He speaks of God freely and often. He seeks opportunities to be alone with God in prayer....
>
> He lives for Others. The Lutheran theologian Dietrich Bonhoeffer calls Jesus the "man for others." What is amazing in Jesus is the universality of his love, his reverence for all persons no matter who they are, his ability to see the good, his desire that all people enjoy inner and outer freedom and fullness of life....
>
> He is the Sacrament of God's Presence, Love and Power. "Emmanuel" is what Matthew's Gospel calls Jesus, "God is with us" (Matt 1:23). In this good man's acceptance of them, people experienced God's own acceptance, forgiveness, and affirmation....
>
> Jesus is Free. The personality of Jesus is original. He is his own person. His replies to questions are fresh, unexpected. His parables are ingenious. His responses to situations are always surprising. Free from other people's expectations....Jesus stays the course, even when it is a very lonely one. He was free from the law and the tradition. He is respectful of both, but Jesus lived a set of values which sometimes required civil disobedience. Jesus was free of possessions. Jesus was free from fear. He continued to do the good and to speak the truth in the face of every threat—of arrest, of calumny, of death.[38]

Hart describes an extraordinary person. This is the stuff of heroes. Combined with Rahner's thought that Jesus is the perfect union of spirit and matter, we encounter in a powerful way the legend that was Jesus of Nazareth. Why would such a person be put to death? Hart sees human brokenness at the heart of it. Ambition, greed, selfishness, and fear drive people to shy away from the good. Envy drives people to reject what is beautiful in others.[39] We are drawn back into the mystery of sin, where destruction is more attractive than awe. Where is God when human beings suffer? In Jesus' life, death, and resurrection the answer is "Emmanuel," God with us. Jesus takes on the suffering of humanity, embracing the pain and hanging on a cross to destroy death.

In taking upon himself the death of the unwanted and unloved, the death of the criminal, the death of the outcast, Jesus confronts the powers that bind humanity to sin. The seductive will to destroy is challenged in the purity of Jesus' act of self-sacrifice. These images of the suffering of Jesus with and on behalf of humanity became very powerful in twentieth-century Europe, torn apart by two world wars. A German theologian, Jürgen Moltmann, became a leading spokesperson for the Christian community reflecting on the Holocaust. Where was God when six million Jews were killed? With Wiesel, Moltmann answered that God was there, suffering:

> The incarnate God is present, and can be experienced, in the humanity of every man, and in full corporeality. No one need dissemble and appear other than he is to perceive the fellowship of the human God with him. Rather, he can lay aside all dissembling and sham and become what he truly is in this human God. Furthermore, the crucified God is near to him in the forsakenness of every man. There is no loneliness and no rejection which he has not taken to himself and assumed in the cross of Jesus. There is no need for any attempts at justification or for any self-destructive self-accusations to draw near to him. The godforsaken and

rejected man can accept himself where he comes to know the crucified God who is with him and has already accepted him. If God has taken upon himself death on the cross, he has also taken upon himself all of life and real life, as it stands under death, law and guilt. In so doing he makes it possible to accept life whole and entire and death whole and entire. Man is taken up, without limitations and conditions, into the life and suffering, the death and resurrection of God, and in faith participates corporeally in the fullness of God. There is nothing that can exclude him from the situation of God between the grief of the Father, the love of the Son and the drive of the Spirit.[40]

Thus Moltmann interprets the cross of Jesus as reconciling humanity, in all of its brokenness, to God. The union of God and human person in the cross breaks down the barriers of ambition, greed, envy, selfishness, and fear that drive humanity away from God. God has assumed human sinfulness and evil in order to help humanity escape sin and evil.

Conclusion

Qoheleth raises the fundamental question: Why do the evil prosper? He understands the spiritual tradition of Israel, which believes that the good are blessed by God. But his experience of life shows him otherwise. This question has at least two prongs: Why does God permit the innocent to suffer? What responsibility does humanity have in this problem? Who is responsible? In this chapter the "accused" is God. We have explored the issue through a set of reflections on theodicies. As a response to evil in the world, we touched briefly on the conclusion that God does not exist. The innocent suffer because there is no benevolent divine being to help them. For Christians, this answer is unsatisfactory.

After examining the basic structure of the problem inherent in any theodicy, we joined the theological discussion of a group of theologians and philosophers who picked the question apart and examined it under the microscope of their own faith, intellect, and sense of morality. They reconnected with the faith of their Christian ancestors. The writings of both Saint Augustine and Saint Irenaeus were presented as inspiration. The reality of human sinfulness and responsibility were brought home in the teachings of Augustine. Irenaeus, an earlier church father and bishop, took a different slant; for Irenaeus, the finite nature of the human creature necessitated moral growth into maturity in order to prepare humanity for union with God. The twentieth-century writers found themselves in different places on the question. Stephen Davis holds humanity responsible for the moral evil in the world, and he revisits the classic teaching that the devil is responsible for physical evil. John Hick supports the notion of divinization, built upon Irenaeus's teaching that we are made in God's image and we have to grow in God's likeness. The overwhelming reality of moral evil compels John Roth to conclude that he must protest against both evil and the God who permits it to go unchecked. David Griffin argues that God cannot overpower humanity and coerce it to conform to moral goodness. Rather, God's power is persuasive. Why does God permit evil? In the end we are faced with the mystery of human reality and the mystery of suffering. Ultimately, it will be our own faith, intellect, and sense of morality that will answer the question.

From a Christian perspective, revisiting the question finds us in the face of the greatest of Christian symbols and realities: the cross of Jesus Christ. The tradition of the Suffering Servant from the Hebrew scriptures connects the spiritual life of the first-century Christians to their scriptural heritage. The tradition of the innocent lamb, led to the slaughter to take on the sins of the many, becomes a theological language for them to understand the meaning of Jesus' death on a cross, a death "he freely accepted." Twentieth-century Jewish writers Elie Wiesel and Harold Kushner continue to find meaning in the symbol of the God who suffers with the people. The Gospel of Mark describes the story of the life and death of Jesus. Jesus sees long before others that his mission will end in a violent death, and he accepts this consequence as necessary in a way that his friends and followers do not and cannot. His birth, the incarnation, is seen through the evolutionary perspective of twentieth-century theologian Karl Rahner. Rahner sees the perfect union of matter and spirit in Jesus. And the death of Jesus on the cross, through Jürgen Moltmann's eyes, becomes a powerful force for the disintegration of evil through the love, the grace, of God.

From here, we move to the other "prong." What responsibility does humanity have for evil? In this chapter we stood in "judgment" to assess God's culpability. In the next chapter we expand our analysis to consider human culpability.

3

Accountability

In 1893 French Catholic lay philosopher Maurice Blondel wrote:

> Yes or no, does human life make sense, and does man have a destiny? I act, but without even knowing what action is, without having wished to live, without knowing exactly either who I am or even if I am. This appearance of being flutters about within me, these light and evanescent actions of a shadow, bear in them, I am told, an eternally weighty responsibility, and that, even at the price of blood, I cannot buy nothingness because for me it is no longer. Supposedly, then, I am condemned to life, condemned to death, condemned to eternity! Why and by what right, if I did not know it and did not will it?[1]

By what right? No one chooses to live, to be born, states Blondel. Individuals discover with growing consciousness that they are alive, are separate and unique, and that they are compelled to respond to their existence by taking up their given life and living it. The mystery Blondel is attempting to unravel is profound. The human person is born without prior knowledge or consent and is then sentenced to a life whose fundamental characteristics are by and large predetermined (historically, socio-economically, biologically, and psychologically). This life, Blondel notes, seems to bear an enormous weight of responsibility and to indicate a destiny that goes beyond the bounds of mortal life.[2] We are condemned to life, death, and eternity? Why?

In this chapter we examine the other side of the question of culpability: What responsibility does humanity have for evil? This raises other issues: Does humanity function within a moral order? Is an individual's human existence measured by a standard of moral perfection? Are we accountable for our lives to God? What are the consequences for failure? If there are consequences, do we experience them immediately? What can be understood about the traditional religious teachings about purgatory and hell?

Does Humanity Function Within a Moral Order?

The operative word here is *conscience*. Human beings have a capacity to discern right and wrong. American civil law is built upon the recognition of conscience. Any accusation of crime assumes a human moral foundation. To kill another human being is murder and is judged to be immoral and unacceptable in society. The capacity to know right from wrong permits the common agreement that murder is wrong. If someone is judged by psychiatrists to be criminally insane, a determination has been made that the person's psyche has a defective conscience. Such a person will not stand trial but be incarcerated in a hospital.

Conscience is a universally recognized human capacity. Its origin is identified by Christians as part of what God intended when human beings were created. In the mid-1960s the bishops of the Catholic Church met in Rome for the Second Vatican Council. As a result of those meetings, a series of documents were produced, one of which was a unique statement of the church's relationship with the world community. In that document the bishops described the fundamental characteristics of the human person in a line of thought intended to find common ground with people around the world. One of those characteristics was "conscience."

Deep within his conscience man discovers a law which he has not laid upon himself but which he must obey. Its voice, ever calling him to love and to do what is good and to avoid evil, tells him inwardly at the right moment: do this, shun that. For man has in his heart a law inscribed by God. His dignity lies in observing this law, and by it he will be judged. His conscience is man's most secret core, and his sanctuary. There he is alone with God whose voice echoes in his depths. By conscience, in a wonderful way, that law is made known which is fulfilled in the love of God and of one's neighbor. Through loyalty to conscience Christians are joined to other men in the search for truth and for the right solution to so many moral problems which arise both in the life of individuals and from social relationships.[3]

The bishops built their description of conscience on scripture. They cited Paul's reference to conscience in his letter to the Romans (2:15–16). A law "written in their heart" guides human actions, although the bishops acknowledge that it is not perfect. One can still be deceived, confused, and act in a way that is sinful.[4] Nonetheless they see this universal conscience as a force within the human person that inspires "the search for truth."

Whether divinely created or not, it seems clear that human beings have a moral order that they recognize and to which they desire to conform. Morality, then, seems to come from within the human person. That moral order becomes a litmus test for life. And for death? Would it not make sense that the human person would expect complete accountability at the end of a long and complex life full of success and failure, courage and weakness, peace and anxiety, clarity and muddle? If each action is evaluated by a law written in the heart, would not the sum total of a life bear a final mark of goodness or evil? How could each decision have a moral character if the whole were never judged? Would it not be contradictory?

For human satisfaction, it seems that every person will be held accountable for his or her life. The question is: when and by whom?

Temporal Retribution and Its Challengers

Why me? This question is often spoken by those who, through no obvious fault of their own, have encountered tragedy or unjust treatment. Ordinary people who work hard, who are kind and responsible, expect life to be good. For many people in the present United States, life really is pretty good. Middle-class people can expect a comfortable home, employment, good schools, family vacations, and movies on a Saturday night. They have plenty to eat, in fact, too much food, and when they get sick they go to the doctor and have access to the medicine they need. The expectation is that "you get what you deserve." If you are a good person, you expect to be rewarded with all of the bounty American life has to hold.

But then, when life doesn't work out well, we complain. Why me? How could I lose my job, when I have worked here for twenty years? How could I miscarry again? How could my husband die of a heart attack at thirty-five? How could my spouse leave me?

In other words, our expectations are based on the principle of temporal retribution. We expect immediate gratification, immediate reward for our goodness. And if we have failed in some way, we expect (or at least fear) immediate punishment. The religious interpretation of temporal retribution attributes the immediacy of results to God. God will punish the wicked and reward the good. Look at that wonderful family! No wonder they are so wealthy. See how strong he is? He must take good care of himself. That old curmudgeon who cheated everyone dropped dead this morning.

He got what he deserved. They fired the guy who stole the files. Good riddance.

This notion of immediacy was a principle of life in ancient Israel. A truly honorable man would be wealthy, with many wives and children, sheep and goats, with land and respect from the community. If tragedy struck, it was because God was punishing him. Sin was a disease not easily cured once it entered the life of a family. The sins of the father could still affect the fortunes of his children. The God of Israel was a God of justice, who meted out punishment to the wicked. The world was in order, and people knew what to expect. Yet those at the bottom of the social world, the least powerful, the poor, somehow were treated gently. Taking care of the widow, the orphan, and the stranger was a moral imperative that recurred in the preaching of the prophets throughout Israel's long history.

Pay attention to this,
  foolish and senseless people
Who have eyes and see not,
  who have ears and hear not.
Should you not fear me, says the LORD,
  should you not tremble before me?
I made the sandy shore the sea's limit,
  which by eternal decree it may not overstep.
Toss though it may, it is to no avail;
  though its billows roar, they cannot pass.
But this people's heart is stubborn and rebellious;
  they turn and go away,
And say not in their hearts,
  "Let us fear the LORD, our God,
Who gives the rain,
  early and late, in its time.
Who watches for us
  over the appointed weeks of harvest."

Your crimes have prevented these things,
   your sins have turned back these blessings from you.
For there are among my people criminals;
   like fowlers they set traps,
   but it is men they catch.
Their houses are as full of treachery
   as a bird-cage of birds;
Therefore they grow powerful and rich,
   fat and sleek.
They go their wicked way;
   justice they do not defend
By advancing the claim of the fatherless
   or judging the cause of the poor.
Shall I not punish these things? says the LORD;
   on a nation such as this shall I not take vengeance?
   (Jer 5:21–29)

The people of Israel expected happiness, wealth, and prosperity to follow goodness. Attention to the poor was an avenue to show one's moral character, thus assuring one's place in life. But what about the poor?

Gustavo Gutiérrez, who speaks for the suffering peoples of Latin America, raises the question of the unmerited misery of the people of Central and South America: "How are we to talk about God… from within a specific situation—namely, the suffering of the innocent?"[5] Gutiérrez studies the Book of Job from that perspective. Why Job? It seems clear to him that the book of Job wrestles with the issue of temporal retribution. Is it really true that God blesses the good with earthly happiness and punishes the evil with misery? The story of Job indicates otherwise. From the comfort of middle-class America to the cardboard shacks in the slums of Lima, Peru, the question persists: How do we assess the moral weight of life and how do we talk about God in the face of human suffering? The question of moral responsibility remains intertwined with the way we speak about God. Gutiérrez reads the Book of Job from the perspective of the "crucified people" of Latin America.[6]

> In this reading of the Book of Job I shall keep my attention on what it means to talk of God in the context of Latin America, and more concretely in the context of the suffering of the poor—which is to say, the vast majority of the population. The poor live their faith and proclaim their hope in the midst of what the Medellín and Puebla episcopal conferences call "inhuman misery" and "antievangelical poverty," resulting above all from unjust social structures that favor a privileged minority. The innocence that Job vigorously claims for himself helps us to understand the innocence of an oppressed and believing people amid the situation of suffering and death that has been forced upon it.[7]

The Book of Job tells the story of a man who lives a good and morally upright life and yet is faced with bitter heartbreak and tragedy. Job gathers with his friends, and they argue, lament, and struggle with the situation. His friends want desperately to believe that there is a reason for Job's suffering, that somehow Job has sinned against God. If that is the case, then repentance will restore peace and happiness to Job. This would also leave intact the moral order they trust, that goodness is rewarded and evil is punished. Job, however, cannot comfort them and help them remain secure in their world. He challenges their assumptions because he will not admit what is not true. Job has his own journey through this suffering into new faith and insight.

The Book of Job

> One day, when the sons of God came to present themselves before the LORD, Satan also came among them. And the LORD said to Satan, "Whence do you come?" Then Satan

answered the LORD and said, "From roaming the earth and patrolling it." And the LORD said to Satan, "Have you noticed my servant Job, and that there is no one on earth like him, blameless and upright, fearing God and avoiding evil?" But Satan answered the LORD and said, "Is it for nothing that Job is God-fearing? Have you not surrounded him and his family and all that he has with your protection? You have blessed the work of his hands, and his livestock are spread over the land. But now put forth your hand and touch anything that he has, and surely he will blaspheme you to your face." And the LORD said to Satan, "Behold, all that he has is in your power; only do not lay a hand upon his person." So Satan went forth from the presence of the LORD." (Job 1:6–12)

The story of Job revolves around a wager. Satan challenges the true moral character of Job, telling the Lord that Job's love and fidelity are shallow. Job is devoted simply because he is happy. If he were suffering, Satan claims, that faith would disappear and be replaced by a virulent hatred. The Lord agrees to test Job to determine the nature of his faith, to see if it is self-serving or disinterested. Unconditional love is the ideal beneath this wager. Can this human being love God (or others, for that matter) for who they are, without asking "what's in it for me?" A series of disasters quickly rob Job of his children and livestock. The Lord points out to Satan Job's faithfulness, for Job does not blaspheme. However, Satan is not satisfied. Satan says that Job will be able to withstand loss as long as it does not affect his own person. If God were to touch his body with disease, then Job would break down and reveal his lack of true faith. God permits this second test:

So Satan went forth from the presence of the LORD and smote Job with severe boils from the soles of his feet to the

crown of his head. And he took a potsherd to scrape himself, as he sat among the ashes. Then his wife said to him,
"Are you still holding to your innocence? Curse God and
die." But he said to her, "Are even you going to speak as
senseless women do? We accept good things from God;
and should we not accept evil?" Through all this, Job said
nothing sinful. (Job 2:7–10)

As Job sees it, good and evil both come from God. Job is willing
to accept what has been given to him by God. His wife is angry
and confused, and assumes that Job will give in to rage and
curse God. He won't do that, but he is indeed miserable. His
three friends, Eliphaz, Bildad, and Zophar, arrive:

They met and journeyed together to give him sympathy and
comfort. But when, at a distance, they lifted up their eyes
and did not recognize him, they began to weep aloud; they
tore their cloaks and threw dust upon their heads. Then
they sat down upon the ground with him seven days and
seven nights, but none of them spoke a word to him; for
they saw how great was his suffering. (Job 2:11b–13)

Job breaks the silence with a lament: "Why did I not perish at
birth?" (3:11) His friends respond in a series of speeches that
escalate into heated debate with Job. Eliphaz states the basic
teaching they have trusted:

Reflect now, what innocent person perishes?
    Since when are the upright destroyed?
As I see it, those who plow for mischief
    and sow trouble, reap the same.
By the breath of God they perish,
    and by the blast of his wrath they are consumed.
    (Job 4:7–9)

Job is wrestling with demons. In his mind he knows that he does not deserve what has happened to him. And he speaks out: "I will complain in the bitterness of my soul" (Job 7:11). This kind of self-defense outrages Bildad, who responds, "How long will you utter such things?...Does God pervert judgment?" (Job 8:2–3) As his friends escalate the argument, searching for sinfulness in Job's life, somewhere, somehow, Job embarks on his own quest. Job wants the Advocate to defend him in a trial before God. He wants justice.

> "But as for me, I know that my Vindicator lives,
> and that he will at last stand forth upon the dust;
> Whom I myself shall see:
> my own eyes, not another's, shall behold him,
> And from my flesh I shall see God;
> my inmost being is consumed with longing.
> (Job 19:25–26)

Job wants to see the face of God, something denied to humanity according to the tradition of the people of Israel. Merely touching the Ark of the Covenant, which held the tablets containing the ten commandments, led to death. No one saw the face of God. But that is what Job demands. The arguments with his friends finally end after Job swears an oath of innocence. A young man, Elihu, arrives. And he humbly asks to speak. Elihu agrees with Job's friends:

> There is no darkness so dense
> that evildoers can hide in it.
> Therefore he discerns their works;
> he turns at night and crushes them. (Job 34:22,25)

Yet, he says that God uses suffering to chastise, to dissuade man from being attracted to evil.

For God does speak, perhaps once,
  or even twice, though one perceive it not.

In a dream, in a vision of the night,
  [when deep sleep falls upon men]
  as they slumber in their beds,
It is then he opens the ears of men
  and as a warning to them, terrifies them;
By turning man from evil
  and keeping pride away from him,
He withholds his soul from the pit
  and his life from passing to the grave. (Job 33:14–18)

Elihu intimates that perhaps Job's sin is one of self-righteousness. What proves Elihu wrong is God, who appears before Job. Now it is God who challenges Job: "Gird up your loins now, like a man; / I will question you, and you tell me the answers!" (38:3) Were you there when I created the world? Have you climbed the highest mountain, plumbed the deepest sea? Did you array the firmaments, make the animals bow to your command? Job responds in complete humility that he is nothing compared to God. The Lord, however, is not satisfied with this statement, and presses Job further. Can you control the forces of chaos? Why don't you then stop those who would do evil: "Let loose the fury of your wrath; / tear down the wicked and shatter them" (40:11–12).

Job responds to God's appearance with awe and gratitude. He states:

I know that you can do all things,
  and that no purpose of yours can be hindered.
I have dealt with great things that I do not understand;
  things too wonderful for me, which I cannot know.
I had heard of you by word of mouth,
  but now my eye has seen you.

Therefore I disown what I have said,
    and repent in dust and ashes. (Job 42:2–6)

The encounter with God was all that Job wanted. He is satisfied to trust that God knows and rules, and that God's powers extend to keeping order in the universe. Interestingly, Gustavo Gutiérrez challenges the translation of this passage, suggesting that the entire meaning of Job's profession of faith has been misunderstood. In Gutiérrez' view Job has undergone a spiritual transformation that is completed with this epiphany of God. Job came to link his own innocent suffering with the lot of the poor. In an impassioned statement Job reveals a stark reality: The misery of the innocent who suffer is inflicted directly and personally by those who would profit from hurting them. Gutiérrez points in particular to Job's seventh reply:

The wicked move boundary-marks away,
    they carry off flock and shepherd.
They drive away the orphan's donkey,
    as security, they seize the widow's ox.
The needy have to keep out of their way,
    poor country people have to keep out of sight.
Like wild desert donkeys, they go out to work,
    searching from dawn for food,
    and at evening for something on which to feed their children.
They go harvesting in the field of some scoundrel,
    they go pilfering in the vineyards of the wicked.
They go about naked, lacking clothes,
    and starving while they carry the sheaves.
Two little walls, their shelter at high noon;
    parched with thirst, they have to tread the winepress.
They spend the night naked, lacking clothes,
    with no covering against the cold.
Mountain rainstorms cut them through,

unsheltered, they hug the rocks.
The orphan child is torn from the breast,
   the child of the poor is exacted as security.
From the towns come the groans of the dying
   and the gasp of the wounded crying for help.
   Yet God remains deaf to prayer!
In contrast, there are those who reject the light;
   who know nothing of its ways
   and who do not frequent its paths.
When all is dark the murderer leaves his bed
   to kill the poor and needy.
During the night the thief goes on the prowl,
   breaking into houses while the darkness lasts.
   (Job 24:2–14, NJB)[8]

Job's desire to see God is founded on his own experience of
suffering as well as the insight he has to the larger issue of the
suffering of the poor. For Gutiérrez, this insight of Job's is
prophetic. It signals clarity of vision. Job seeks an encounter with
God to make sense of life, to confirm the goodness and mercy of
the Lord of his faith. Temporal retribution makes no sense, based
on his experience and the life of the innocents who suffer. When
he encounters God, Job is filled with peace. Gutiérrez says this
discovery leads Job to repent with dust and ashes, that is, to give
up his lament.[9] What has he learned? Gutiérrez writes:

Only when we have come to realize that God's love is
freely bestowed do we enter fully and definitely into the
presence of the God of faith. Grace is not opposed to the
quest for justice nor does it play it down; on the contrary,
it gives its full meaning. God's love, like all true love, oper-
ates in a world not of cause and effect but of freedom and
gratuitousness.[10]

Beyond Temporal Retribution: Hell and Purgatory

From our discussion of the Book of Job and a twentieth-century commentary by liberation theologian Gustavo Gutiérrez, it seems clear that justice is not meted out step by step, action for action, throughout the course of life. In fact, violence, oppression, hatred, and injustice deeply affect the quality of life for many people. Job—and Gutiérrez—felt confident, just as the ancient Israelites did, that God "heard our cry and saw our affliction, our toil and our oppression" (Deut 26:7). Confident in God's loving presence, the people of Israel and centuries of Christians have trusted in that love and mercy. Other worldviews have replaced the notion of temporal retribution, and in Christian history we see the development of a belief in hell, and within the Catholic tradition a belief in purgatory.

The existence of hell is presumed in the New Testament. The wicked are punished with eternal torment in hell. The devil, under many names and identities, such as Satan and Lucifer, along with his many henchmen, are damned to hell, and their reign of torment creates their own misery as well as the agony of hell's inhabitants. The fall of the angels is described in the visions of Enoch, apocryphal texts dating from the third century B.C.[11] Enoch sees what is in store for the fallen angels, who have corrupted humanity through their own lust and desire for bloodshed, war, and destruction. For the earth, God will send the flood to destroy all that they have created, saving Noah and his family to start again. As for the fallen angels, they will be imprisoned forever.

And from thence I went to another place, which was still more horrible than the former, and I saw a horrible thing: a great fire there which burnt and blazed, and the place was cleft as far as the abyss, being full of great descending columns of fire: neither its extent or magnitude could I see, nor could I conjecture. Then I said "How fearful is the place and how horrible to look upon!" Then Uriel answered me, one of the holy angels who was with me, and said unto me, "Enoch, why hast thou such fear and affright?" And I answered: "Because of this fearful place, and because of the spectacle of the pain." And he said unto me: "This place is the prison of the angels, and here they will be imprisoned for ever." (XXI. 7–10)...

And thence I went to another place, and he showed me in the west another great and high mountain of hard rock....Then Raphael answered, one of the holy angels who was with me, and said unto me: "These hollow places have been created for this very purpose, that the spirits of the souls of the dead should assemble therein, yea that all the souls of the children of men should assemble here. And these places have been made to receive them till the day of their judgement and till their appointed period, till the great judgement." (XXII.1.3–4)...

This division has been made for the spirits of the righteous, in which there is the bright spring of water. And this has been made for sinners when they die and are buried in the earth and judgement has not been executed upon them in their lifetime. Here their spirits shall be set apart in this great pain, till the great day of judgement, scourgings, and torments of the accursed for ever, so that there may be retribution for their spirits. There He shall bind them for ever. (XXIII. 9–11)[12]

Enoch's visions describe scenes of primeval history, when angels, spiritual beings unrelated to humanity, abandoned their ethereal existence to invade human society. The skeletal description in Enoch's writings indicates that corruption and destruction result. In response, these fallen angels are forever banned from God's presence. Their destiny of darkness and torment is witnessed by Enoch. A similar fate awaits the sinners.

The devil appears in the Gospel of Matthew as tempter, to test the mettle of Jesus. After his baptism, Jesus is led into the desert, where he fasts for forty days and nights.

> The tempter approached and said to him, "If you are the Son of God, command that these stones become loaves of bread." He said in reply, "It is written:
> 'One does not live by bread alone,
>   but by every word that comes forth
>   from the mouth of God.'"
> Then the devil took him to the holy city, and made him stand on the parapet of the temple, and said to him, "If you are the Son of God, throw yourself down. For it is written:
> 'He will command his angels concerning you'
>   and 'with their hands they will support you,
>   lest you dash your foot against a stone.'"
> Jesus answered him, "Again it is written, 'You shall not put the Lord, your God, to the test.'" Then the devil took him up to a very high mountain, and showed him all the kingdoms of the world in their magnificence, and he said to him, "All these I shall give to you, if you will prostrate yourself and worship me." At this, Jesus said to him, "Get away, Satan! It is written:
> 'The Lord, your God, shall you worship
>   and him alone shall you serve.'"
> Then the devil left him and, behold, angels came and ministered to him. (Matt 4:3–11)

Jesus' ability to withstand the devil's temptations is hailed by Paul in his writings. He calls Jesus "the new Adam," the one who could resist sin in a way that Eve and Adam could not. Jesus acknowledged the presence of demons as he exorcised them from their victims. Jesus preached the good news of God's love and forgiveness and called for repentance and faith. He recognized the moral weight placed on humanity, and spoke of the Last Judgment.

> When the Son of Man comes in his glory, and all the angels with him, he will sit upon his glorious throne, and all the nations will be assembled before him. And he will separate them one from another, as a shepherd separates the sheep from the goats. He will place the sheep on his right and the goats on his left. Then the king will say to those on his right, "Come, you who are blessed by my Father. Inherit the kingdom prepared for you from the foundation of the world. For I was hungry...and you gave me drink, a stranger and you welcomed me, naked and you clothed me, ill and you cared for me, in prison and you visited me." Then the righteous will answer him and say, "Lord, when did we see you hungry and feed you, or thirsty and give you drink? When did we see you a stranger and welcome you, or naked and clothe you?..." And the king will say to them in reply, "Amen, I say to you, whatever you did for one of these least brothers of mine, you did for me." Then he will say to those on his left, "Depart from me, you accursed, into the eternal fire prepared for the devil and his angels. For I was hungry and you gave me no food, I was thirsty and you gave me no drink, a stranger and you gave me no welcome, naked and you gave me no clothing, ill and in prison, and you did not care for me." Then they will answer and say, "Lord, when did we see you hungry or thirsty or a stranger or naked or ill or in prison, and not minister to your needs?" He will answer them, "Amen, I say to you, what you did not do for one of these least ones, you did not

do for me." And these will go off to eternal punishment, but the righteous to eternal life. (Matt 25:31–46)

The way to eternal life is through sharing in the love of God for all of humanity, especially those who are suffering. Those who fail to love will meet the same fate as the devil and his angels: eternal fire. Jesus strongly challenges his listeners to transform their lives. His sermons and parables paint pictures of human life lived to the fullest, rich with love, generosity, and self-sacrifice. The New Testament writings also record his death, Jesus' personal confrontation with evil, and his resurrection. These actions are intended to reunite humanity with God, heal the rupture caused by human sinfulness, and combat the destructive force of the fallen angels.

The early Christians accepted the worldview portrayed in the New Testament. They took seriously the seductive and treacherous effort of the devil and the threat of hell for sinners. Western culture, art, and literature explored and expanded on the history of the fallen angels and the torments of hell. Late-twentieth-century authors documented the historical development of belief in the devil and hell by examining not only the dogmatic church teachings, theological writings of pastors, Protestant and Catholic, and theologians, but also the popular culture of ordinary people's beliefs and practices. Most striking, perhaps, is the research and comparison of beliefs expressed by artists, poets, playwrights, sculptors, and painters who created vivid and graphic representations. Their art and writing influenced one another. Several key images emerged from these sources.

Geographically, hell was located in the bowels of the earth. There existed a tradition that the islands of Ireland and Sicily were points on the earth where one could access these lower regions and enter purgatory, a region of the netherworld, according to Catholic belief and practice, where repentant sinners endured punishment in atonement for their sins before entering heaven. Beneath purgatory was hell. This geography of hell was not challenged until the Enlightenment. Vision narratives exist over the course of Christian history in the West by individuals who thought they experienced or imagined this world of suffering and torment. Certainly the most famous journey through hell, purgatory, and heaven is *The Divine Comedy* by Dante (1265–1321). Two centuries earlier an Irish monk had written *The Vision of Tundale*. Alice Turner notes in *The History of Hell* that "nearly 250 hand-lettered manuscripts in at least fifteen languages survive, and one is fully illustrated by Simon Marmion, including eleven scenes of Hell. Nothing else like it exists for vision literature, though there is another miniature of Tundal's Hell in the most famous of all medieval breviaries, *Les Tres Riches Heures* commissioned by Jean, Duke of Berry, from the Limbourg brothers in about 1413."[13] Tundale, in the depths of hell, describes Satan as a "horrible monster."[14]

> The prince of darkness, the enemy of the human race…was bigger even than any of the beasts he had seen in hell before….For this beast was black as a crow, having the shape of a human body from head to toe except that it had a tail and many hands. Indeed, the horrible monster had thousands of hands, each of which was a hundred cubits long and ten cubits thick. Each hand had twenty fingers, which were each a hundred palms long and ten palms wide, with fingernails longer than knight's lances, and toenails much the same. The beast also had a long, thick beak, and a long, sharp tail fitted with spikes to hurt the damned souls. This horrible being lay prone on an iron grate over burning coals fanned by a great throng of demons….This enemy of the human race was bound in all his members and joints with iron and bronze chains burning and thick….Whenever he breathed, he blew out and scattered the souls of the damned throughout all the regions of

hell....And when he breathed back in, he sucked all the souls back and, when they had fallen into the sulphurous smoke of his maw, he chewed them up....This beast is Lucifer and he is the first creature that God made.[15]

The damned souls of hell are tortured by Satan and his henchmen, the demons. The souls have bodies that experience the physical pain of fire and ice, of ripped flesh, disembowelment, and decay. Smells of the most wretched kind and screams of agony fill the darkness. Images of naked bodies contorted with pain fill the canvases and frescoes of Christian art work. Punishment is specific to the crime. Sins of adultery, homosexual expression, and fornication are portrayed in some of the paintings of hell as punished with perverse sexual torments, the like of which our modern culture would term pornographic. The eternal pain of the damned was portrayed as a necessary part of the plan of salvation. Why? The "abominable fancy"[16] was a part of the joy of the blessed, that is, to be able to witness this miserable suffering. The parable of Lazarus and the rich man was used to support this assertion.[17]

When the poor man died, he was carried away by angels to the bosom of Abraham. The rich man also died and was buried, and from the netherworld, where he was in torment, he raised his eyes and saw Abraham far off and Lazarus at his side. (Luke 16:22–23)

The stench of hell and the misery of the damned are images used by preachers to warn Christian believers of their fate if they engage in sinful conduct. Fear of hell, of fire and brimstone (sulphurous smoke), was used as a tool to enforce morality. The damned would be in hell for all eternity. There would never be an end to their suffering. The overwhelming power of this time frame was intended to strike fear in the heart of sinners, terrifying them into repentance. Fear of hell was part of the spirituality of ordinary Christian faith throughout the centuries of Christian history.

The persistence of these images of Satan and hell, writes D. P. Walker, can be attributed to the "very strong scriptural authority for the doctrine. But a more fundamental reason for the long triumph of hell was the firm and almost universal belief in its value as a deterrent in this life. It was thought that, if the fear of eternal punishment were removed, most people would behave without any moral restraint whatever and that society would collapse into an anarchical orgy."[18] This fear of "orgy," of riotous and perverted sexual conduct, historians tell us, is rooted in European fear of witchcraft. Jeffrey Burton Russell states that devil worship as seen in the United States in recent years is frivolous compared to the suspected practices of witches in the years from 1400 to 1700:

By the fifteenth century a stereotype of diabolical witchcraft had emerged: on a Thursday or Saturday night, some men, but more women, crept silently from their beds in order to avoid disturbing their spouses. The witches who are near enough to the meeting place make their way on foot, but those who live at a distance rub their bodies with an ointment that enables them to fly off in the shape of animals, or else astride broomsticks or fences. Ten or twenty witches attend the meeting, later called a "sabat." The ceremony begins with any new witches swearing to keep the group's secrets and promising to kill a child and bring its body to the next meeting. The neophytes renounce the Christian faith and insult a crucifix or Eucharistic host. They proceed to worship the Devil or his representative by kissing his genitals or backside. After the initiation, the witches bring children to be sacrificed to the Devil, and the babies' fat is used to confect the ointment used for flying or for poison. The witches partake of the child's body and blood in a blasphemous parody of the Eucharist. After supper, the lights are extinguished, and the witches fall to an indiscriminate sexual orgy, sometimes having intercourse with the Devil himself.[19]

Like all stereotypes, this one is a caricature. The witch hunts in Europe and America were more often than not scapegoating in societies incapable of absorbing change, difference, and tragedy; "the willingness to assume that those whom one distrusts or fears are servants of Satan and fitting targets of destruction," thought Russell, leads to a moral breakdown of society with tragic consequences.[20] The image of the witch as murderer, cannibal, and slut was powerful. Whatever its basis in reality through the Reformation, it kept the reality of the devil alive and terrifying, and made an impression on European history. In late-nineteenth-century writings there is evidence of black Masses in Paris, with perverse sexual behavior taking place while the eucharistic host was desecrated.[21]

Images of such depravity were heavy on the mind of people like Matthew Horbery, who in 1744 wrote:

The great Argument for working out our Salvation in the present Life, while it is called today, is, because the Night cometh, when no Man can work. But if Men are once taught to believe that there will be Another Day, that will answer their purpose as well; it is natural to think, that they will be too apt to trust to that Resource, and so live and die without Repentance. I don't say that this Conduct would be reasonable, but that it is likely to be Fact, considering how strongly Men are attach'd to their old and favourite Sins....It should seem that it is the Eternity of the Punishment, which gives its chief Weight and Edge, and makes it pierce deepest into the Hearts of Sinners. It is the

Notion that That miserable State will admit of neither
Remedy, nor End, that alarms their Fears, that restrains
their Wickedness within some bounds, and is most likely
after all to make them repent of it. It seems natural to think
it must be so in Reason, and it evidently appears to be so
in Fact.[22]

This practical use of the eternity of hell as a deterrent, argued Walker,
led to intense intellectual wrestling with the rise of seventeenth-
century rationalism.[23] In support of deterrence many intellectuals
compromised their objections to this image of hell in order to
protect the so-called weak-minded or loose-moralled. Walker's
research on the subject entailed searching through unpublished
writings of such major figures as Sir Isaac Newton (1642–1727)
to discover their true thoughts and feelings on hell. A conspiracy
of silence seemed to dominate, as social and political ostracism
was quick and severe for those who dared to question the belief.
Nonetheless, the objections that emerged were substantive. The
belief necessitated a static state in hell; those punished could not
grow, change, or repent, for if they did, why could they not be
saved? How could the finite sins of a human being bring on eternal punishment? Eternal torment served the purpose of vindictive justice, that is, violent punitive retribution for whatever
crimes had been committed. But how could such driving vindic-
tiveness be reconciled with Christianity? The Protestant theology
of predestination seems to place responsibility for hell in God's
hands, not humanity's. And finally, after the Final Judgment
what further use would hell as a deterrent have? They were also
struggling with the sheer numbers of people said to be damned,
for the New Testament references are always to the more difficult
journey of true faith that few have the strength and courage to
follow. Limbo, a place of natural happiness where unbaptized
babies would go for all eternity, since they would not be able to
experience the beatific vision, was also questioned: "Since infant

mortality has until recently been extremely high, it is reasonable to suppose that dead babies constitute at least 50% of the total population of the dead. As Horbery says, 'one half of our species die, perhaps, before they have actually committed any Sin to deserve the Damnation of Hell.'"[24] These substantive challenges to hell had a significant impact on the intellectual and spiritual culture of Western Europe and the developing Americas. Even the geography of hell was challenged. Based on growing scientific information, new theories were postulated. Tobias Swinden, in 1714, suggested that hell was really the sun, whose fire and enormity could encompass the mass of sinners.[25] William Whiston, after studying both Newton's theories and the work of Edmund Halley on comets, theorized that the icy and fiery conditions of comets would be an appropriate environment for hell. This was not well received by the other members of the Royal Society.[26]

The images we have discussed in this chapter—the Devil, the torments of hell, the damnation of sinners, the evil magic of witches, and Satan's efforts to tempt and destroy—have not moved far from modern consciousness or belief. In the *Catechism of the Catholic Church* the eternity of hell is still accepted.

> The teaching of the Church affirms the existence of hell and its eternity. Immediately after death the souls of those who die in a state of mortal sin descend into hell, where they suffer the punishments of hell, "eternal fire." The chief punishment of hell is eternal separation from God, in whom alone man can possess the life and happiness for which he was created and for which he longs. (no. 1035)[27]

Nonetheless, the catechism also asserts that God wills all to be saved and none to enter hell unless he or she willfully turns from God (no. 1037). A choice made against God has also emerged in moral theology, where it is called the fundamental option. This option is made by the individual at death, either for life, for God, or against God, choosing eternal separation. Still, many people, it seems, continue to believe in an eternal hell: "According to a recent Gallup poll, 60 percent of Americans believe in Hell or say they do, up from 52 percent in 1953. Only 4 percent think they're likely to go there."[28] In a way, that is the fundamental argument used to refute the eternity of hell: Most people cannot really believe that their sins justify eternal punishment. As Marie Huber argued in 1731, the punishment does not fit the offense: "Let a Schoolmaster tell his Scholar that his Father will hang him, if he doth not study; he laughs at the menace."[29] Perhaps the Catholic belief in the purification of the soul after death, purgatory, has persisted since its crystallization in the late Middle Ages because it responds to the problem of the lack of temporal retribution as well as the issue of eternal punishments for humanity's finite sins.[30]

Purgatory shared geographical territory with hell. It has been imaged as "a place" through much but not all of its development. Dante described it as a mountain in his epic *Purgatorio*. Jacques Le Goff comments in *The Birth of Purgatory*:

It is not hard to understand why one bit of natural geography attracted particular attention when it came to locating the site of Purgatory, or at least the mouths of Purgatory, on earth: volcanoes. As mountains they spit fire from a crater or pit at the center, these had the advantage of combining three key physical and symbolic ingredients of Purgatory's structure. We shall see presently how men roamed Sicily between Stromboli and Etna hoping to compile a map of Purgatory. But in Sicily there was no group capable of taking advantage of the opportunity offered by the local geography; by contrast, the Irish, their English neighbors, and the Cistercians who organized carefully controlled pilgrimages to the site of Saint

Patrick's Purgatory were able to do this. The problem with Frederick II's Sicily was that it had a sovereign suspected of heresy, Greek monks, and Moslem inhabitants and so was thought to be insufficiently "catholic" to be the site of one of Purgatory's main portals. Mount Etna, moreover, had a long association with Hell, which proved difficult to overcome.[31]

Le Goff is alluding to Frederick II (1215–50), who is remembered by historians as "one of the fascinating personalities of the Middle Ages. Indeed his modern conception of kingship, his ruthless application of power in political affairs, his religious skepticism, his broad cultural interests, the splendor of his cosmopolitan court in Sicily; all of these things have led historians to name him the first 'Renaissance man.'"[32] The medieval competition for the site of an entrance to purgatory seemed to favor Ireland, where it was believed that Saint Patrick through a revelation found an entrance. At that spot a church was built, which stands today, located on Station Island in Lough Derg, County Donegal; "from the thirteenth century onwards the belief was widespread that whoever spent twenty-four hours in the 'cave' or 'pit' of the Purgatory would be exempt from purgatory after death."[33]

The origins of purgatory were found in scripture. In the history of the Maccabean Revolt of the Israelites in 165 B.C., Judas Maccabeus and his soldiers were burying their dead after a battle when they found "amulets sacred to the idols of Jamnia, which the law forbids the Jews to wear" (2 Macc 12:40). They prayed together, and then Judas

> took up a collection among all his soldiers, amounting to two thousand silver drachmas, which he sent to Jerusalem to provide for an expiatory sacrifice. In doing this he acted in a very excellent and noble way, inasmuch as he had the resurrection of the dead in view; for if he were not expecting the fallen to rise again, it would have been useless and

foolish to pray for them in death. But if he did this with a view to the splendid reward that awaits those who had gone to rest in godliness, it was a holy and pious thought. Thus he made atonement for the dead that they might be freed from this sin. (2 Macc 12:43–46).[34]

Le Goff notes that the medieval mind would naturally find a correlation between an Old Testament teaching and a New Testament teaching. In the case of purgatory, the parallel is in the writings of Saint Paul:[35]

No one can lay a foundation other than the one that is there, namely, Jesus Christ. If anyone builds on this foundation with gold, silver, precious stones, wood, hay, or straw, the work of each will come to light, for the Day will disclose it. It will be revealed with fire, and the fire [itself] will test the quality of each one's work. If the work stands that someone built upon the foundation, that person will receive a wage. But if someone's work is burned up, that one will suffer loss; the person will be saved, but only as through fire. (1 Cor 3:11–15)

The theological rationale for a belief in purgatorial fires, and in purgatory, evolved over the course of Christian history. It was sustained by vision narratives, accounts by saints who experienced or witnessed to its reality. One of the early martyrs, Perpetua, recorded a vision in A.D. 203 of her brother in purgatory; he was released from his suffering through her prayers.[36] The sayings and teachings of the fifteenth-century mystic Saint Catherine of Genoa (1447–1510) were collected in several texts, in one of which she states that she experienced purgatory "in the flesh":

While still in the flesh this blessed soul experienced the fiery love of God, a love that consumed her, cleansing and purifying all, so that once quitted this life she could appear forthwith in God's presence.[37]

Based on her experiences, Saint Catherine wrote:

> The will of the souls in purgatory…
>   is in all respects in conformity with that of God.
> That is why God responds to their goodness with His,
>   thereby cleansing them of actual and original sin.
> As for blameworthiness,
>   those souls are as pure as when God created them,
>   since in leaving this world they grieved for their sins
>   and were determined to sin no more.
> It is this sorrow over their sins
>   that makes God forgive them,
>   so that the only thing remaining in them
>   is the rust and deformity of sin,
>   which fire then purifies.
> Once completely purified,
>   having become one with God's will,
>   these souls, to the extent that God grants them,
>   see into God.[38]

The teachings of the Council of Trent (1563) solidified the beliefs about purgatory, expressed in scripture and in the experience and writings of Christians over the centuries. At the twenty-fifth session the bishops issue the *Decree Concerning Purgatory*.

> Whereas the Catholic Church, instructed by the Holy Ghost, has, from the sacred writings and the ancient tradition of the Fathers, taught in sacred councils, and very recently in this oecumenical Synod, that there is a Purgatory, and that the souls there detained are helped by the suffrages of the faithful, but principally by the accept-

able sacrifice of the altar ["Wherefore, not only for the sins, punishments, satisfactions, and other necessities of the faithful who are living, but also for those who are departed in Christ, and who are not as yet fully purified, is it rightly offered." Session XXII, Chapter II]. (Session XXV)[39]

The economy of salvation, in Catholic experience, created a communion not only of saints, earthly and heavenly, that allowed for their mutual aid, but this aid reached those who were suffering in purgatory, being purified in preparation for union with God.

It is important to note, nonetheless, that this doctrine was controversial and did not pass through the Protestant Reformation unscathed. Martin Luther, the spiritual leader of the Reform movements that inaugurated Protestantism, objected to the doctrine. He wrote

God has, in his Word, laid before us two ways; one which by faith leads to salvation,—the other, by unbelief, to damnation.

As for purgatory, no place in Scripture makes mention thereof, neither must we any way allow it; for it darkens and undervalues the grace, benefits, and merits of our blessed, sweet Saviour Christ Jesus.

The bounds of purgatory extend not beyond this world; for here in this life the upright, good, and godly Christians are well and soundly scourged and purged.[40]

Luther could not accept a system of purgation that seemed to ignore the power and efficacy of the life, death, and resurrection of Jesus. Nor would he recognize the efficacy of the ongoing "sacrifice" of the Mass. Indeed, questions could be raised about purgatory that had been raised about hell. What is the fundamental reality of Jesus, if so much further repentance and purgation needs to be accomplished by Christians? Did Jesus die once, or does he die every time a Mass is offered? Why would his death be necessary? What effect did it have? Why does hell or purgatory exist at all, after the resurrection of Jesus? Did he not descend into hell itself to free its prisoners?

Conclusion

In this chapter we have focused on the question of human responsibility for evil. The human capacity to discern right and wrong, conscience, is a clue that human beings hold themselves accountable for their actions. The brokenness and sinfulness of human behavior are internally unacceptable. That human beings would one day be fully accountable for the whole of their lives follows naturally from this power of conscience. When and how human beings experience judgment, reward, and punishment became the next point of discussion. The Book of Job and its commentary by Gustavo Gutiérrez represent a tradition within Judaism and Christianity, that temporal retribution, the immediate effects of moral actions, is not the lived reality of ordinary people. The suffering of the innocent echoes through the centuries in Christian spirituality as a rupture in God's plan for humanity. The development of belief in hell followed Christian experience. We considered the strongest images that endured through the centuries of Satan and the torments of the damned. Purgatory, a Catholic dogma and belief, represents one dimension of Christian teaching on judgment and the afterlife. The teachings on hell and purgatory are not free of controversy and difficulty. They raise problems about the role of Jesus' life, death, and resurrection. These questions will be addressed again in chapter 5. We turn now, though, to a most important question: What is the fate of the blessed?

4

Happiness

The glory of Him who moveth everything
Penetrates the universe, and shines
In one part more, and in another less.
Within that heaven which most receives His light
I have been, and seen things past the knowledge
Or power of any who comes back to tell—
Because, as it approaches its desire,
Our intellect so deepens as it seeks,
That memory has not the power to follow.
As much, however, of the holy realm
As I have treasured up within my mind,
Shall now become the subject of my song.[1]

What is the fate of the blessed? Life is brief, and death is certain. What lies beyond for those whose lives are filled with love, charity, and self-sacrifice? Our questions about heaven are manifold. How does heaven relate to this life? Is eternal existence superior and disconnected from the toils and tribulations of this world? Is it so different that one would forget about human existence? Or does heaven complement, build, and fulfill human existence? If human existence pales before the power and happiness of heaven, why is there so much intensity to this life, such sweet joy, such bitter sorrow? If heaven completes and perfects human existence, how can it "fix" memories, for example, the death of a child or the brutality of abuse? If life after death connects into our experience on earth, what if our life was miserable and inadequate, no education, no love, no meaning? Does growth and change occur after death, as transformation? Who will we be in heaven? Will our sense of self continue? Will our gender, race, ethnicity, personality, and knowledge persist? What is the nature of the afterlife? Is eternal life rooted in the reality of an immortal soul? Is there a resurrection of the body? What kind of bodiliness could persist after natural death? Where is heaven? When we look at the night sky through a telescope, it is nowhere to be found. Shouldn't we be able to sense the presence of life in the universe? Where are fifty billion people going to go? What are they going to do, when they get there? Does time persist in eternity? What is the nature of eternal life?

The mystery of life is tied to questions of ultimate meaning: What is the purpose for human existence, and what is our destiny after death? In this chapter, we explore the myriad facets of these questions about heaven.

Hoping for Heaven

The human race has pondered the meaning of its existence ever since it became conscious. We could examine the great literature from ancient cultures and find questions about the meaning of life and death. From our perspective, within the Christian tradition, we will begin with a gospel story that raises these issues: the story of the raising of Lazarus (John 11). Lazarus, the brother of Jesus' friends Martha and Mary, lies dying in Bethany, a small town two miles from the city of Jerusalem. When he falls ill, Martha and Mary send word to Jesus to come to Bethany to heal him. Although he receives the message, Jesus delays his departure two days. When he announces to the disciples that he is heading for Judea, they argue with him, telling him that he will surely be killed. Jesus' decision is not swayed, and Thomas says then, "Let us also go to die with him" (John 11:16). When Jesus arrives, Lazarus has been dead and buried four days. Martha hears that he is coming and goes out to greet him on the road. She says:

> "Lord, if you had been here, my brother would not have died. [But] even now I know that whatever you ask of God, God will give you." Jesus said to her, "Your brother will rise." Martha said to him, "I know he will rise, in the resurrection on the last day." Jesus told her, "I am the resurrection and the life; whoever believes in me, even if he dies, will live, and everyone who lives and believes in me will never die. Do you believe this?" She said to him, "Yes, Lord. I have come to believe that you are the Messiah, the Son of God, the one who is coming into the world." (John 11:21–27)

Martha has faith in a future resurrection. At the time that Jesus lived, some Jews did not believe in individual life after death, the immortality of the soul of the Greco-Roman world, or the resurrection of the body. Belief in individual resurrection emerged late in Israel's history, probably during the time of the Maccabee brothers, 150–100 B.C. Some, like Martha, believed in an afterlife. The Last Day would be a day of judgment. Jesus not only supports Martha's hope in a resurrection but also invites her to trust that he is the way toward that life in God. Jesus then joins Mary and the friends who have gathered; he goes to the tomb and asks that the stone be rolled back. Martha protests because Lazarus has been dead for four days and the odor will be overwhelming. Jesus prays and calls Lazarus by name. Lazarus emerges from the tomb, once again alive. And what is the response of the witnesses? "Now many of the Jews who had come to Mary and seen what he had done began to believe in him. But some of them went to the Pharisees and told them what Jesus had done....So from that day on they planned to kill him" (John 11:45–46, 53). The miracle of Lazarus being raised from the dead did not necessarily bring faith to the observers. Those who protested Jesus' message and purpose drew no solace from this act. Rather, they chose to interpret it as a further outrage against the Torah and to use it to plot his death. Jesus raises Lazarus from the dead, and through this act he hastens his own death; it is the last straw in his confrontations with the Jewish authorities, and they decide that Jesus must die. "I am the resurrection and the life," says Jesus, but the path to life must move first through death.

The message of resurrection is controversial. Jesus must combat the traditionalist thinking of the Sadducees, the priestly aristocracy who control worship in the Temple.[2] They have rejected the possibility of resurrection because they believe it is not part of the teachings of the Torah. In the Gospel of Mark, the Sadducees challenge Jesus on this question. They set up a scenario: What would happen if a woman were married seven times, to one brother after another, following Levirate law for a woman who has no child, whose wife would she be in heaven? (cf. Mark 12:18–23). Jesus states:

> "Are you not misled because you do not know the scriptures or the power of God? When they rise from the dead, they neither marry nor are given in marriage, but they are like the angels in heaven. As for the dead being raised, have you not read in the Book of Moses, in the passage about the bush, how God told him, 'I am the God of Abraham, [the] God of Isaac, and [the] God of Jacob'? He is not God of the dead but of the living. You are greatly misled." (Mark 12:24–27)

The ultimate confrontation, though, is the passion, the torture and death of Jesus on a cross. All four of the gospels contain narratives that describe Jesus' arrest, torture, crucifixion, and burial as do other nonbiblical sources (e.g., Josephus, Suetonius,

Tacitus, and Pliny the Younger).[3] Jesus died on a cross, of this there is ample evidence. His death is not the end, however.

There are accounts in the gospels of a tomb found empty by Mary Magdalene, followed by encounters with the risen Jesus. Some of these experiences take place in Jerusalem, and others in Galilee.

> After the sabbath, as the first day of the week was dawning, Mary Magdalene and the other Mary came to see the tomb. And behold, there was a great earthquake; for an angel of the Lord descended from heaven, approached, rolled back the stone, and sat upon it. His appearance was like lightning and his clothing was white as snow. The guards were shaken with fear of him and became like dead men. Then the angel said to the women in reply, "Do not be afraid! I know that you are seeking Jesus the crucified. He is not here, for he has been raised just as he said. Come and see the place where he lay. Then go quickly and tell the disciples, 'He has been raised from the dead, and he is going before you to Galilee; there you will see him.' Behold, I have told you." Then they went away quickly from the tomb, fearful yet overjoyed, and ran to announce this to the disciples. And behold, Jesus met them on their way and greeted them. They approached, embraced his feet, and did him homage. Then Jesus said to them, "Do not be afraid. Go tell my brothers to go to Galilee, and there they will see me." (Matt 28:1–10)

The tradition of the New Testament witnesses to Jesus' continued existence after his crucifixion and burial. There are six accounts in the gospels that describe Jesus appearing to his followers in Galilee and in Jerusalem. The above account of Jesus appearing to his followers conforms to a basic pattern described by Dermot Lane:

1. The circumstances of the appearances are the same in that the followers of Jesus are despondent and disappointed. "But we had hoped that he was the one to redeem Israel." [As Jesus died, his followers were already dispersing, convinced that Jesus' ministry was a failure and fearing for their lives. They did not expect him to rise from the dead.]

2. The initiation for the appearances comes from Jesus. "Jesus came and stood among them." [Jesus suddenly is there. Lane and others talk about the uniqueness of these appearances. Jesus has not come back to life as his friend Lazarus did, and although he is seen in a body it does not quite conform to the physical limits of ordinary existence. He can be seen and touched, in the encounter in Jerusalem he could eat, yet he appears and disappears.]

3. There is some form of greeting from Jesus. [In this case "Peace be with you."]

4. A moment of recognition follows. [The followers are first shocked and unable to respond. Jesus must coax them into trusting what they are experiencing.]

5. A command of Jesus concludes the appearance. "Go therefore and make disciples." [Jesus' mission will continue through the work of his followers, who are charged with the responsibility of preaching in his name.][4]

What can be said of the resurrected Jesus? He appears to his disciples in a transformed state. His body seems to have some ordinary traits, like his ability to eat, but he does not simply return to a human existence. Jesus is present to his followers, but he does not stay with them. The resurrection stories occur within a limited time frame and conclude with Jesus' final ascension.

The resurrection of Jesus inspired the early church to preach the good news of salvation. It was convincing enough to rally his despondent followers to believe again and to carry on the difficult mission that lay ahead. It strengthened the frightened followers enough for them to risk death; many eventually sacrificed their lives for the sake of the gospel. The resurrection of Jesus was central to the preaching of the early disciples. When Peter stood up at Pentecost to speak to the crowd, he said:

> "You who are Israelites, hear these words. Jesus the Nazorean was a man commended to you by God with mighty deeds, wonders, and signs, which God worked through him in your midst, as you yourselves know. This man, delivered up by the set plan and foreknowledge of God, you killed, using lawless men to crucify him. But God raised him up, releasing him from the throes of death, because it was impossible for him to be held by it." (Acts 2:22–24)

This story in the book of Acts indicates that many who heard Peter that day felt compelled by his words and accepted baptism (Acts 2:37–41). However, that was not universally true. When Paul spoke in the Areopagus to the citizens of Athens, the response was mixed: "When they heard about the resurrection of the dead, some began to scoff, but others said, 'We should like to hear you on this some other time.' And so Paul left them. But some did join him, and became believers'" (Acts 17:32–34). Walter Kasper used the expression "believing seeing" to describe the original followers' response to Jesus.[5] It was not an experience that overwhelmed those present, forcing them to acquiesce. Rather, it was an invitation. Those who believed shared their faith with others.

From within the Christian tradition, then, we see that the followers of Jesus wrestled with the same questions as other people of their times. The Old Testament is rooted in the Exodus experience of a people who experienced a God who saved them from oppression and brought them to a land filled with milk and honey. That trust in God endured through every kind of torment and persecution and seems to have incorporated a belief in individual happiness after death. At the time of Jesus the Greco-Roman culture permeated the Middle East and the followers of Jesus were exposed to the notion of the immortality of the soul. And yet, the Christians held fast to a belief in the resurrection of the body, in spite of the opposition of the Sadducees and of the Greeks and Romans to this teaching. Confidence in the resurrection was rooted in the early Christian experience of the resurrected Jesus, a witness that is passed on through the gospel narratives.

Faith in the resurrection, body and soul, would become the focus of Christian teaching about death and the afterlife. New Testament writings, and in particular the theological writings of Paul, articulate a vision of the future neither identical with nor completely contrary to the dominant beliefs of the culture. Twentieth-century Lutheran theologian Oscar Cullman has drawn two significant conclusions from Paul's writings: First, Paul believed immortality was achieved through the Christ event, not by its own right; and second, Paul preached the resurrection in the context of the transformation of the world.[6] Cullman focused on Paul's First Letter to the Corinthians:

> But now Christ has been raised from the dead, the first fruits of those who have fallen asleep. For since death came through a human being, the resurrection of the dead came also through a human being. For just as in Adam all die, so too in Christ shall all be brought to life, but each one in proper order: Christ the first fruits; then, at his coming, those who belong to Christ; then comes the end, when he hands over the kingdom to his God and Father, when he has destroyed every sovereignty and every authority and power. For he must reign until he has put all his enemies

under his feet. The last enemy to be destroyed is death. (1 Cor 15:20–26)

Paul's theological argument was based on the story of Adam and Eve. Life on earth was distorted by the sins of our ancestors, bringing suffering and death to the human race. For Paul, Jesus' life and death repaired the damage caused by Adam, and the reign of Christ would then destroy death's hold over the human race. Cullman saw a distinction here, between the Greco-Roman acceptance of death as a natural part of human existence and Christian belief, which rebelled against it.[7] Paul's vision of the afterlife included the transformation of all of creation:

> I consider that the sufferings of this present time are as nothing compared with the glory to be revealed for us. For creation awaits with eager expectation the revelation of the children of God; for creation was made subject to futility, not of its own accord but because of the one who subjected it, in hope that creation itself would be set free from slavery to corruption and share in the glorious freedom of the children of God. We know that all creation is groaning in labor pains even until now. (Rom 8:18–22)

Creation has also been bound up with death, and so for Paul the resurrection of the children of God is only a part of the perfection to come. This idea was central to Cullman's study of New Testament thought on the afterlife: "In reality, does it not belong to the greatness of our Christian faith, as I have done my best to expound it, that we do not begin from our personal desires but place our resurrection within the framework of a cosmic redemption and a new creation of the universe?"[8] What might "cosmic redemption" mean? In the Book of Revelation, a vision narrative written during an era of persecution in the early church, a battle ensues between Christ and the forces of evil, in which Christ triumphantly conquers and claims the earth. Christ's victory creates "a new heaven and a new earth. The former heaven and the former earth had passed away" (Rev 21:1). A new heaven and a new earth became an image of the afterlife for the early church. All of existence would be healed and changed through Christ. This connected with the prophecies in the Old Testament of a time when peace would reign on earth, when all of life would become more than the natural order had determined. The prophet Isaiah wrote:

> But a shoot shall sprout from the stump of Jesse,
>   and from his roots a bud shall blossom.
> The spirit of the LORD shall rest upon him:
>   a spirit of wisdom and of understanding,
> A spirit of counsel and of strength,
>   a spirit of knowledge and of fear of the LORD,
>   and his delight shall be the fear of the LORD.
> Not by appearance shall he judge,
>   nor by hearsay shall he decide,
> But he shall judge the poor with justice,
>   and decide aright for the land's afflicted.
> He shall strike the ruthless with the rod of his mouth,
>   and with the breath of his lips he shall slay the wicked.
> Justice shall be the band around his waist,
>   and faithfulness a belt upon his hips.
>
> Then the wolf shall be a guest of the lamb,
>   and the leopard shall lie down with the kid;
> The calf and the young lion shall browse together,
>   with a little child to guide them.
> The cow and the bear shall be neighbors,
>   together their young shall rest;
>   the lion shall eat hay like the ox.
> The baby shall play by the cobra's den,
>   and the child lay his hand on the adder's lair.

There shall be no harm or ruin on all my holy mountain;
> for the earth shall be filled with knowledge
>> of the LORD,
> as water covers the sea. (Isa 11:1–9)

Writing of his hope for the messiah, Isaiah expressed his vision of the peace and justice that the messiah would bring to Israel. Christians, rereading these prophecies in the light of their experience of Jesus, came to understand that the future promises of salvation would encompass the suffering world, which also needed transformation.

For the early Christians, hoping for heaven meant trusting in the power of Christ's resurrection. That resurrection was wrought from the suffering and death of Christ, and so the church held onto the sense that death was real, fully experienced by the totality of the person, and that what saves humanity is dying in Christ and rising in Christ. The soul was truly and naturally embodied, and after death the soul and body would reunite. Salvation was envisioned to include all of creation, which led them to anticipate a Second Coming, called the *parousia* (from the Greek), when Christ would return to rule the earth and prepare it for the reign of God. Biblical scholars discuss the fact that even in the first years of the church there was confusion over the time of Jesus' return. Some thought that Jesus would return within a generation, and so when the apostles began to die there was confusion in the community. In Second Peter, a text that many scholars date in the second century, concerns were raised about the delay of the parousia:

> In the last days scoffers will come [to] scoff, living according to their own desires and saying, "Where is the promise of his coming? From the time when our ancestors fell asleep, everything has remained as it was from the beginning of creation."...

But do not ignore this one fact, beloved, that with the Lord one day is like a thousand years and a thousand years like one day. The Lord does not delay his promise, as some regard "delay," but he is patient with you, not wishing that any should perish but that all should come to repentance. (2 Pet 3:3–4, 8–9)

Hoping for heaven, the early Christians had to contend with events they had not foreseen, with disappointments and frustrations when the Kingdom did not end the era of suffering that tormented them. Over time, Christian theology would deal with the time between an individual's death and the day of judgment by postulating interim states. One early attempt was made by Origen, a Greek father of the church, who died in A.D. 254. He speculated about the possibility of the transmigration of souls.

Transmigration of Souls

Early theological speculation about the afterlife included a wide array of ideas. Origen, a respected and yet controversial theologian of the third century, postulated the preexistence of souls:

Whole nations of souls are stored away somewhere in a realm of their own, with an existence comparable to our bodily life, but in consequence of the fineness and mobility of their nature they are carried round with whirl of the universe. There the representations of evil and of virtue are set upon before them; and so long as a soul continues to abide in the good it has no experience of union with a body. But by some inclination towards evil these souls lose their wings and come into bodies, first of men; then through their association with the irrational passions, after the allotted span of human life they are changed into beasts;

from which they sink to the level of insensate nature. Thus that which is by nature fine and mobile, namely the soul, first becomes heavy and weighed down, and because of its wickedness comes to dwell in a human body; after that, when the faculty of reason is extinguished, it lives the life of an irrational animal; and finally even the gracious gift of sensation is withdrawn and it changes into the insensate life of a plant. From this condition it rises again through the same stages and is restored to its heavenly place. On earth by means of virtue souls grow wings and soar aloft, but when in heaven their wings fall off through evil and they sink down and become earthbound and are mingled with the gross nature of matter.[9]

The passage of time in Christian history was not only a theological question but a lived reality. How was the ongoing movement of life to be interpreted in light of Christ's promises of the coming of the kingdom? Origen argued that the passage of time lent itself to the moral development of humanity; human beings through their own actions rose to heavenly life as souls or sank through stages of the loss of life on earth. The passions that human life evoked were hard to master, and thus it was possible to see how long a struggle humanity would have to free itself of them. The passage of time, in Origen's case over two hundred years of time since the death of Christ, had affected Christian thought significantly. Note the dichotomy between soul and matter that filtered into Origen's worldview. Matter had become the antithesis of spirit, falling in line with Greco-Roman thought.

If we look back on the writings of Plato, a Greek philosopher of enormous influence who lived from 427–347 B.C., this fundamental example of dualism can be seen in the *Phaedo*:

There is likely to be something such as a path to guide us out of our confusion, because as long as we have a body and our soul is fused with such an evil we shall never adequately attain what we desire, which we affirm to be the truth. The body keeps us busy in a thousand ways because of its need for nurture. Moreover, if certain diseases befall it, they impede our search for the truth. It fills us with wants, desires, fears, all sorts of illusions and much nonsense, so that, as it is said, in truth and in fact no thought of any kind ever comes to us from the body. Only the body and its desires cause war, civil discord and battles, for all wars are due to the desire to acquire wealth, and it is the body and the care of it, to which we are enslaved, which compel us to acquire wealth, and all this makes us too busy to practice philosophy. Worst of all, if we have leisure for some investigation, everywhere in our investigations the body is present and makes for confusion and fear, so that it prevents us from seeing the truth.

It has been shown to us, that, if we are ever to have pure knowledge, we must escape from the body and observe matters in themselves with the soul by itself. It seems likely that we shall only then, when we are dead, attain what we desire and whose lovers we claim to be, namely, wisdom, only after death.[10]

Origen, a Greek, was influenced by the culture in which he lived. His teaching on the transmigration of souls was never accepted into the doctrine of the church. Nonetheless, knowledge of Origen's teaching persisted over time. Even as far away as Tibet in the twentieth century, Tenzin Gyatso, the fourteenth Dalai Lama, the spiritual leader of Buddhists, commented on Origen's teachings in his discussions with Christians about Buddhist philosophy of consciousness and rebirth. In his autobiography, *Freedom in Exile,* the Dalai Lama describes Buddhist belief about rebirth:

Consciousness...flows on and on, gathering experiences and impressions from one moment to the next. At the point of physical death, it follows that a being's consciousness contains an imprint of all these past experiences and impressions, and the actions which preceded them. This is known as karma, which means "action." It is thus consciousness, with its attendant karma, which then becomes "reborn" in a new body, animal, human or divine.... Buddhists further believe that because the basic nature of consciousness is neutral, it is possible to escape from the unending cycle of birth, suffering, death and rebirth that life inevitably entails, but only when all negative karma has been eliminated along with all worldly attachments. When this point is reached, the consciousness in question is believed to attain first liberation and then ultimately Buddhahood. However, according to Buddhism in the Tibetan tradition, a being that achieves Buddhahood, although freed from Samsara, the "wheel of suffering," as the phenomenon of existence is known, will continue to return to work for the benefit of all other sentient beings until such time as each one is similarly liberated.[11]

The passage of time in history, for those of us who have long adjusted to the delay of the parousia, is what we are accustomed to experiencing. Perhaps in our times it is more difficult to imagine that there are those who expect history to come to an end. It is worthwhile to add to this discussion on the nature of the human soul the teachings of Saint Thomas Aquinas, a thirteenth-century father of the church whose influence is unparalleled in Catholic thought.

Saint Thomas Aquinas on the Resurrection

In book four of his treatise *Summa Contra Gentiles* Aquinas discusses the resurrection.[12] He states:

> The souls of men are immortal. They persist, then, after their bodies, released from their bodies. It is also clear from what was said in Book II that the soul is naturally united to the body, for in its essence it is the form of the body. It is, then, contrary to the nature of the soul to be without the body. But nothing which is contrary to nature can be per-petual. Perpetually, then, the soul will not be without the body. Since, then, it persists perpetually, it must once again be united with the body; and this is to rise again. Therefore, the immortality of souls seems to demand a future resur-rection of bodies....The soul separated from the body is in a way imperfect, as is every part existing outside of its whole, for the soul is naturally a part of human nature. Therefore, man cannot achieve his ultimate happiness unless the soul be once again united to the body, especially since it was shown that in this life man cannot arrive at his ultimate happiness.[13]

Aquinas begins with the fundamental belief of the immortality of the soul. In some ways we can see that this is a theological development, for in the early writings of the church, as we have discussed above, the immortality of the soul was not a starting point. Nonetheless, Aquinas sees that the soul is immortal. He then argues that the soul belongs with the body, and it will not persist in eternity separated from the body. In chapter 81 Aquinas argues that the resurrection of the body is possible through divine power and not through the natural order of the universe, for the body ages, dies, and decays after death, accord-ing to the laws of nature. Only through divine power could the body be restored after death.[14] In the following chapters Aquinas addresses a wide array of issues related to the soul and body. Interestingly, although he accepts the immortality of the soul, he does not align himself with any notion of its preexistence before birth (such as Origen believed). For Aquinas, the soul is created by God at conception:

> Again, the soul and body appear to be related in a different order in the first generation of man and in his resurrection. Now, in the first generation the creation of the soul follows the generation of the body, for, when the bodily matter is prepared by the power of the separated seed, God infuses the soul by an act of creation. But in the resurrection the body adapted to the pre-existing soul. Of course, that first life which man acquires by generation follows the condition of the corruptible body in this: man is deprived of that life by death. Then, the life which man acquires by resurrection will be perpetual according to the condition of the incorruptible soul.[15]

According to Aquinas, the soul is infused into the body after conception. This act supports belief in the complete uniqueness of every individual human being, which later generations of Christians came to believe wholeheartedly.

Aquinas wrestled with many questions about the nature of the body after the resurrection. He wondered about the central unity of the body, its nature, its age, and its functioning. Flesh and bones would be recreated after the resurrection, not spiritual bodies, he argued. Yet that flesh and bone would not grow, change, age, or diminish. It would use neither food nor drink, nor would human beings engage in sexual intercourse. He argued that the internal organs would remain, in order to protect the integrity of the body, but they would no longer function. He was particularly concerned about the implications of the possibility of conception and birth after the resurrection; it was inconceivable to him that "human beings" would be created after ordinary life was over. That defied his understanding of the basic nature of humanity. "One ought, nevertheless, not hold that among the bodies of the risen the feminine sex would be absent, as some have thought."[16] The nature of the human race to be both male and female would endure, after the resurrection, according to Aquinas, and further, "the frailty of the feminine sex is not in opposition to the perfection of the risen. For this frailty is not due to a shortcoming of nature, but to an intention of nature."[17] Women are biologically different from men, and that biological distinction is protected after the resurrection, otherwise the reunion of soul with body would be inadequate. The soul could not be united to a different kind of body. As he struggled with these many issues, Aquinas also decided that the age of the person after the resurrection was relevant. He thought that "the age of Christ, which is that of youth," was the perfect age.[18]

Aquinas argued strongly for the resurrection of the body, so that the immortal soul could be restored to its wholeness. For him, the many complicated issues raised with the resurrection of the body were solvable. The opposite, an immortal bodiless soul, was unacceptable.

We have so far discussed the idea of death and resurrection, and the possibility of an afterlife. We have focused on the death and resurrection of Jesus as recorded in the gospel narratives and the early writings of the new Christians. The ongoing belief in an afterlife and the survival of the individual soul have dominated Christian belief and practice over the centuries. But the Christian community has not been univocal on these questions. We could point to early twentieth-century biblical scholarship, in particular the work of Rudolf Bultmann, who called into question the reality of Jesus' resurrection. In late-twentieth-century American Catholic theology Rosemary Radford Ruether has spoken from a feminist perspective on the question of the endurance of the self after death. "This concept of the 'immortal self,' survivable apart from our particular transient organism, must be recognized, not only as untenable, but as the source of much destructive behavior toward the earth and other humans."[19] Peter Phan, a Vietnamese American Catholic theologian writing on Ruether's eschatology, maintains that, for Ruether, the concept of the immortality of the soul emerged because men were afraid of death.[20] Phan notes this passage as central to her thinking:

> Our existence as an individual organism ceases and dissolves back into the cosmic Matrix of matter-energy out of which new centers of individual beings arise. It is this Matrix, and not the individuated centers of being, which is everlasting, which subsists underneath the coming to be and passing away of individual beings.[21]

This brief summary of Ruether's writings on the question of the immortality of the soul serves to remind us that questions remain. Thus we need to bear in mind that human ponderings on the nature of death and the afterlife call us on a fundamental level to a personal stance. Our explorations on the question of the immortality of the soul and the resurrection of the body will broaden in the next section to include a discussion of the purpose and nature of heavenly existence.

The Beatific Vision

Aquinas's influence on Christian belief in the afterlife extends beyond his discussion of the resurrection of the body to include larger questions on the nature of heaven. What does the fullness of resurrection, body and soul, bring to the human person? For Aquinas, heaven meant the experience of seeing God face to face. This biblical image can be seen in the Book of Job, where Job states: "But as for me, I know that my Vindicator lives, / and that he will at last stand forth upon the dust; / Whom I myself shall see: / my own eyes, not another's, shall behold him, / And from my flesh I shall see God; / my inmost being is consumed with longing" (Job 19:25–26). I shall see God with my own eyes, states Job.

Zachary Hayes, an American Catholic theologian, points to several passages in the New Testament that support this sense of longing for an encounter with God, an encounter in which we see God face to face.[22] There is a long history within the Christian tradition that ultimate human happiness in heaven derives from this encounter with God, the *beatific vision*. Our happiness lies in our communion with God. In his summary of the historical background of the church's belief in the beatific vision, Hayes points to the text from the fourteenth-century Council of Florence, which states: "The souls of those who have committed no sins at all after the reception of baptism, and the souls of those who have committed sin but have been purged either while in the body or after they have left the body behind…are taken immediately into heaven and clearly see God himself, one and three, as he is; some more perfectly than others in accordance with the diversity of their merits."[23]

Human persons without sin are brought into communion with God, whom they now experience directly. This is possible, Aquinas argues, because

the ultimate beatitude of man consists in the use of his highest function, which is the operation of the intellect. Hence, if we suppose that a created intellect could never see God, it would either never attain to beatitude, or its beatitude would consist in something else beside God; which is opposed to faith. For the ultimate perfection of the rational creature is to be found in that which is the source of its being; since a thing is perfect so far as it attains to its source. Further, the same opinion is also against reason.

For there resides in every man a natural desire to know the cause of any effect which he sees. Then arises wonder in men. But if the intellect of the rational creature could not attain to the first cause of things, the natural desire would remain vain. Hence it must be granted absolutely that the blessed see the essence of God....Of those who see the essence of God, one sees Him more perfectly than another. This does not take place as if one had a more perfect likeness of God than another, since that vision will not be through any likeness. But it will take place because one intellect will have a greater power or faculty to see God than another. The faculty of seeing God, however, does not belong to the created intellect naturally but through the light of glory, which establishes the intellect in a kind of *deiformity*, as appears from what is said above. Hence the intellect which has more of the light of glory will see God more perfectly. But he will have a fuller participation of the light of glory who has more charity, because where there is greater charity, there is the more desire, and desire in a certain manner makes the one desiring apt and prepared to receive the object desired. Hence he who possesses the more charity, will see God the more perfectly, and will be the more beatified.[24]

The pervasive influence of Aquinas's thought on the nature of heavenly happiness can be seen in a nineteenth-century treatise on heaven written by Jesuit F. I. Boudreaux.[25] Boudreaux begins his discussion of heaven by describing the beatific vision as "a perfect and permanent state" achieved through three inseparable acts of knowing, loving, and enjoying God.[26] He raises concerns about those who would overemphasize the joy of perfected human relationships and pleasures in heaven, to such an extent as to overlook or diminish the centrality of human happiness as an encounter with God. The "error consists in ignoring or making little of the Beatific Vision, after the resurrection, and letting our mind pass from creature to creature, gather exquisite pleasures from each, until practically we make man's happiness in heaven come almost exclusively from creatures."[27] Such pleasures, of communion with the saints and angels, are real and true, but exist within the larger view of our communion with God. In fact, he treats the social joys of heaven in chapter 11 of his text. There he describes six personal attributes to our social intercourse: "virtue, learning, beauty, refinement, mutual love, and the ties of kindred."[28] Our social experiences will be purified; in eternity they will be free of all of the anguish, jealousy, competition, suffering, and inequities that plague ordinary human society. According to Boudreaux, life in heaven brings us peace, rest, intellectual pleasure, and love, transforming and completing our human experiences.

> We now have perfect peace with God, of whose love for us we no longer doubt, as we may have often done when on earth. We also have peace with ourselves; for those unruly passions which formerly disturbed our peace, no longer exist in our glorified bodies. We enjoy perfect peace with our neighbor; for conflicting interests, envies, and jealousies, which gave rise to dissensions and enmities, have not found and never will find their way into heaven. We also have peace from the devil, who no longer "goeth about like a roaring lion, seeking whom he may devour." He has found no admittance into the kingdom of peace. We also have peace from our past life; for the sins which so often made us tremble, are washed away in the blood of Jesus, and are, therefore, no longer a source of trouble. The remembrance of them rather intensifies our for the God of mercy, and therefore increases our happiness. We now, also, have peace from our future. That awful future was formerly shrouded in impenetrable darkness, and often filled

us with gloomy forebodings. But now the judgment is over;...we now gaze undismayed into that bright outspread eternity, wherein we see nothing that can ever disturb our peace.[29]

Rest and intellectual pursuits are especially filled with joy for human beings who spent their lives in poverty, toil, and oppression. Now they can fulfill the longings of their minds and bodies for joy, knowledge, and rest. And last, Boudreaux talks of the inadequacy of our human experience of love, in contrast with basking in the light of the love of God and the saints in heaven:

Think of this, ye mortals, who crave after human love. You desire to love and be loved. Love is the sunshine of your lives. But, do as you will, it can never give you perfect happiness here below; for when you have, at last, succeeded in possessing the object after which you so ardently sighed, you discover in it imperfections which you had not suspected before; and these lessen your happiness. But suppose, even, that you are one of the few who are as happy as they expected to be, how long will your blessedness last? A few years, at most. Then, death, with a merciless hand, tears way from you the objects of your love. Is not this the end of all earthly happiness? Look up to heaven, and there see the Blessed in the presence of God. They are as happy to-day in their love as they were hundreds of ages ago.[30]

From the distance of several hundred years an American Jesuit priest continued to find inspiration in the medieval imagery and theology of heaven constructed by Aquinas and others. Zachary Hayes points out, though, that in Aquinas's time, his was not the only perspective; "The basic, unifying act for those who follow Thomas Aquinas is that of the intellect (= vision). For those following Scotus, on the other hand, the basic unifying act is that of will (= love)."[31] Nonetheless, union with God became the central vision of the afterlife.

A Place in Heaven

Colleen McDannell and Bernhard Lang point to tensions between theocentric and anthropocentric visions of heaven that shadow Christian thought through the centuries. From the medieval period there has been a dichotomy between the Scholastic theologians and the mystics and monks in their images of heaven. McDannell and Lang state that monks preached a vision of heaven as the new Eden and as medieval cities grew the new Jerusalem; mystics, inspired by the Song of Songs, anticipated union with Christ, while Scholastic theologians spoke of intellectual fulfillment and the vision of God.[32] The theology of Saint Thomas became the public belief of the church, while the mystical traditions were passed on in the spirituality of religious life.[33] Then came the Renaissance:

> The new dignity of "worldly" occupations and the Ciceronian hope of meeting friends reshaped the traditional Christian views of eternal life. Renaissance authors and artists found medieval views of heaven uncongenial to the mentality of their day and thus unsatisfactory. Given its emphasis on the beatific vision, scholastic teaching did not allow for the development of the human side of heaven. Renaissance theologians and artists made up for these deficiencies by envisaging a twofold heaven, one that would take account of God's majestic presence and also give the redeemed their due as creatures with independent dignity....Just as God's earthly home is the church, his heavenly home is the celestial city. The saints enter God's city not to live but to worship....The paradise garden of heaven is different, but no less dignified part of heaven....Trees,

birds, flowers, and meadows flourish.... People touch, play, listen to music, and pass eternity in pleasure.[34]

But the exuberance and joyful imaginings of heaven of the Renaissance were brought up short as Europe moved into the Reformation and the Catholic Counter-Reformation. Vestiges of their humanism remained in the memory of Christianity, in particular the notion of reuniting with friends and loved ones.[35] Christian images of heaven continued to fluctuate between God-centered and family-and-friends-centered spirituality, between contemplation and mission, between passivity and productivity. There was tremendous diversity in thought, belief, and spirituality as Western culture moves through the centuries.

Where Is Heaven?

Obviously, the history of Christianity on the "what" of heaven remains conflicted, but what of the "where?" Where is heaven? Looking within the origins of Western culture, it is possible to trace a pattern of the development of a geography of heaven, beginning with the Greco-Roman world. Christian images of heaven were built upon the broader culture, and in particular on the work of Aristotle. Jeffrey Burton Russell outlines the progression of thought:

The sense that up is better was common in ancient Near Eastern religion. In Greco-Roman thought it was reinforced by Aristotle's physics. Christian philosophers adopted his system, especially as refined by the geographer Ptolemy (second century CE). In this system the universe consists of nested, or concentric, spheres. (No educated person believed the world was flat.) At the center of the cosmos is the sphere of the earth, surrounded by a sphere of air and, above that, a sphere of "purer air," called *ether*. Above the ether were the planetary spheres. Encircling the earth in ascending order were the spheres of the moon, Mercury, Venus, the sun, Mars, Jupiter, and Saturn. Beyond them were, first, the sphere of the fixed stars and then, the outer skin of the cosmos, the sphere of the *primum mobile*, which imparted rotation and all movement to the spheres under it. Ptolemy first posited the primum mobile to account for irregular movements of the eighth sphere, the slight movement of the stars owing to the procession of the equinoxes. The cosmos is thus a great sphere containing all spheres.

In this system, adopted by Christianity and later employed by Dante, any movement from the earth is by definition both outward and upward motion....The classical and preclassical religious background imparted the idea that as one approached the primum mobile, the spheres grew purer, less material and more spiritual. Down at the center, the earth is the deepest, densest, darkest, most material place in the universe. Heavy elements such as water and earth sink naturally downward, while air moves naturally upward, and fire strives to reach up beyond air to the ether and beyond. Past the outermost sphere, the primum mobile, is the empyrean, the place of pure fire (Greek *pyr*). The soul's true home, like that of light and fire, is in the empyrean with God....

Although the name "empyrean" derives from *pyr*, fire, it is called that not because it burns but because it shines *(non ab ardore, sed a splendore)*, terms that later delighted Dante. It is a body, although a divine rather than a natural one, a quintessential one, a fifth body differing from every other body in that there is nothing outside or beyond it that limits or defines it. Unmoved, it moves the cosmos.[36]

The medieval cosmos was depicted by Schedel in the *Nurem-berg Chronicle* (1493). Robert Hughes states that the spheres in

Schedel's diagram show the earth at the center, with its "girdles of water, air and fire. Next, the seven spheres of the planets, followed by the 'firmament'—where the Zodiac revolved—which was separated by the 'crystal heaven' from the *Primum Mobile*, the source of universal movement. Beyond the *Primum Mobile* was the Empyrean,...crowded with God and his saints."[37] Interestingly, Hughes wrote, the medieval concept of the girdle of fire that rings the earth "corresponds roughly to the Van Allen radiation belt of modern science."[38]

What can be said, then, in the light of these imaginings, about the "where" of heaven? It seems clear that a long tradition in Western culture has held onto a view of the universe that incorporates the basic astronomy and physics of earlier times. The universe is larger than the earth and visible stars and planets— of this they were convinced. God, the source of being and creation, exists beyond the visible, natural world, uncontrolled and undetermined by its laws. Ideas about the nature of God have always included the negatives: God is not physical, God is not limited, God is not..., God is not.... In the medieval view of heaven, the empyrean was defined as a fifth essence, a category beyond those of earth, air, fire, and water. Where was heaven? It was not on earth, although as we have discussed, some thought hell was in the core of the earth and some thought purgatory was. Heaven is "up above." These medieval concepts of heaven envisioned humanity, raised from the dead, in the empyrean with God.

This medieval cosmology imagines eternity in paradise as far removed from any earthly contact or concern. The question raised by Saint Paul about the transformation of the world, re-created anew through the coming of Christ, is set aside. Is it our destiny to be completely unconnected in this manner? German Catholic theologian Karl Rahner, writing in the early 1960s on the question of death, posed this question. Is our eternal existence "acosmic?" Rahner suggests that perhaps after death we remain in communion with the world, with humanity as it lives on in time and space on earth after our death; perhaps this reality of presence rather than absence is conceivable. Rahner suggests that perhaps the human person is "pancosmic":

> In its lifetime, the soul-animated body is an open system in relation to the world, and that in natural philosophy it is not so easy to regard the human body as ending at the skin. Moreover, the spiritual soul through its embodiment is in principle open to the world and is never a closed monad without windows, but is always in communication with the whole of the world....Such a relation of the soul to the world, if it is not exaggerated into a repetition of its earlier relationship to its own body, might imply that the soul, by surrendering its limited bodily structure in death, becomes open towards the universe and, in some way, a co-determining factor of the universe precisely in the latter's character as the ground of the personal life of other spiritual corporeal beings. We know as a doctrine of faith that the moral quality of each individual human life, when consummated before God, becomes co-responsible for his attitude towards the world and towards all other individuals; in a somewhat similar sense, the individual person, once rendered pancosmic through death, by this real ontological and open relation to the whole cosmos, might come to have a direct influence within the world.[39]

So there is more to consider here, in our ruminations about the "where" of heaven: Is it the medieval empyrean or a transformed and transforming world where humanity stays bound together, spirit and flesh, as the world continues its own course, its own destiny?

Conclusion

In this chapter we have considered questions about the destiny of the blessed. We began our study by considering gospel stories that portray Jesus' teachings about death and resurrection, as well as his own journey that moves through death into new life. We read of the struggles of the early Christians both to believe in the resurrection and then to spread the good news of salvation. Their hopes for Jesus' quick return to transform all of life were set aside as time passed. We then addressed questions about the nature of the soul, the relationship between the soul and body, and the meaning of the resurrection of the body. Our probing continued, examining the idea of the beatific vision as a way to describe the nature of the resurrected life. And finally, we looked to find a place where heaven could be. We ended with the open-ended wonderings of Karl Rahner on the possibility of a continued presence of the human person to the world. We turn now to the second part of the task before us. Much like a puzzle with many pieces, in these four chapters we have organized, categorized, and grouped together pieces that interrelate, and now we must complete the puzzle. In some manner we must find a way to fit the pieces together, to form a whole that makes sense, that makes life make sense, that will give us the courage and vision to make all of the little choices day to day that make up the story of our lives. With death as our horizon, we must answer these questions, for ourselves, if for no one else.

PART TWO
Constructing a Personal Response

5

Life in the Face of Death

In the face of modern-day ambiguity, the burden of creating meaning and remaining faithful to one's beliefs lies clearly within the purview of the individual. Perhaps only in the early life of the church have Christians existed in similar conditions, caught between open hostility and complete indifference. The magnitude of life's problems and challenges does not diminish simply because answers are not forthcoming. On all sides we are pressed to make sense out of life, make decisions that have enormous consequences, and live within limits that we have not set. How then, should we act?

In this last chapter I attempt to respond to the questions raised in Part One. I share with you a statement of faith, my faith. And I encourage you to do the same. For in the final analysis, what is important is how you make sense of life, not how I do.

Death as Our Horizon

My earliest spiritual awakenings revolved around the power of death. I was afraid. I would imagine myself in a grave, trapped in a decaying body, still conscious, still attached to it. These imaginings were so real to me that I would break out in a cold sweat. By the time I was a student in college, I sought out individuals who seemed to be able to confront death. Perhaps my whole life has been a quest for peace in the face of my own mortality. I know that I stand with giants as I say that, the epic poets, the great philosophers. But really, I stand with each and every human being. We all can sense this wall, this end, long before it is a reality. It is something that we share, one and all.

The why of death must be linked with the why of life; if I knew who I was, and why I am alive, I might be able to understand why I am going to die. Perhaps, though, these two questions will be answered simultaneously; that is, in the face of death, I will come to know who I am. It seems to me that the mystery of life is intertwined with the mystery of death. As time goes by, and now I am more than midway through my life, I find fewer answers to the why of my life. When I was younger, I felt I had a calling from God, a unique purpose in the world, a destiny and a responsibility to fulfill. Now I feel just hints that perhaps a little piece of my life is just what God had in mind. And somehow, for reasons I can't explain, this is enough.

Perhaps becoming a parent has taught me to accept death. I see the next generation coming along, and the need to make way for it. In Chapter 1 I discussed the myth of Adam and Eve. Were they destined for an eternity on earth? Are we? As I see it, eternity does not belong in space and time on earth. All of life—the seas, trees, rabbits, and flowers—exists in the present, in concrete yet transitory ways. The symbolic meaning of human sinfulness conveyed in the story of Adam and Eve cannot really overshadow the physical realities we know. Scientists can show us the tracings of our past, evidence of a world and a universe in formation. We have dinosaur skeletons in museums and chairs in astrophysics in universities. We know a great deal about the how of things, just not the why. I find Steven Hawking's willingness to acknowledge the limits of scientific knowledge refreshing. And it reminds me of the duties those of us in theology and ministry have to be meaning-makers, probing and building for the sake of the community. The path of evolutionary development leaves open the possibilities that we dream of when we speak of heaven. We look to the transformation of the world and a life to come. Given the progress of the universe in time, why are such expectations unreasonable?

Life is a greater mystery than anything else we know. And so is God. I find that a great comfort. I can live with a mystery that is so great it takes my breath away. Perhaps it would have been exciting to have been given more power and knowledge of this world, like the prophets and visionaries we read about in the history of Christianity. Indeed, when I was young, that was my ambition. And yet, I can see the value of what I do know, and I can live with what I do not.

Unraveling the mysteries that surround our lives, I find the story of Jesus Christ compelling. For me, making sense of life involves connecting my story with his story. Within the life of one human being we find the imprint of God in an extraordinary and unique way. The human goodness of Jesus foreshadows our own ability to become loving and beautiful people. His healing touch, his perceptiveness and goodness, his ability to give to others and ultimately to give himself for others, these traits are more than admirable, they are signs of the power of life within all of us. We should think of Christ from within an evolutionary perspective, or so thought Karl Rahner.[1] What is the meaning of the union of God and human being in Jesus? It was simple for Rahner. The course of evolution can be seen as a movement of matter toward spirit. And in that evolutionary movement, the human being holds a unique place. The human spirit has evolved to a place of self-possession and self-transcendence, making it possible for the human being to rise up, moving toward union with God.[2] Human beings, imbued with the divine spirit, made in the image and likeness of God, have within them the power of movement toward God and eternity. Is this believable? I think so.

We can't talk about death without talking about life. Some things are clear. We can sense our common bonds with the world around us, with the plants and trees and stars, and yet we can also sense our differences. Self-possession and self-awareness make us different. Of course we are completely intertwined with our physical selves, and our bodily existence defines us in so many ways—our sex, our race, our experiences in time and history. But we remember the past, live in the present, and dream of the future. We can transcend the moment, we can transcend experience and pain, we can live for a future that has yet to happen. That ability to transcend the moment, to transcend our own needs and desires, has created the heros and saints we celebrate and remember. How many of us in out own ordinary life have done the right thing at great personal cost? I think we all have. Every time a child is born, there is a life at risk, a woman in pain. I come from a family of firefighters, ordinary people who walk into burning buildings. We can love our lives, cling to who we are and what we have, and yet risk it all, give it away in an instant, for the sake of one whose need is greater. As human beings, we have this capacity for self-transcendence. Rahner argued that this power of self-transcendence is the strength that enables us to move toward God, who moved toward us. He described this spiritual strength as a gift from God, as part of the life offered to us in birth. As individuals, we bring power and beauty into our lives. And yet we never stand alone. As a human family, we perdure.

Through the ravages of history, through war and desolation, we have survived. "You can crush the flowers, but you can't stop the spring,"[3] said the people of El Salvador during a period of terrible tragedy and violence. We can't make sense of life if we don't see ourselves as unique individuals and as intimately bound to one another. Our questions about happiness and heaven often express our longing to stay connected to the ones we love. Our yearning for love and communion is a part of the mysteries that encompass us. We want to live not only for ourselves but with one another. It is not enough to be alive; we long for life in the presence of others. For those whose religious sensibilities have developed, we long for union with that divine presence we sense, with God.

The vast complexity and diversity of the world become more and more apparent the closer we are bound together in this modern world of telecommunication. At times it is confusing, even frightening, to experience people whose lives are fundamentally different from our own. Religious difference has been at the root of wars and violence throughout human history; we can't seem to face the threat of seeing God from another perspective. Nor can we seem to stand differences in race, culture, language, and gender. We hurt and oppress, or are oppressed, for our differences. I think that we are in another evolutionary transition. This is a new challenge for the human race that will not go away. We must come to grips with our differences, not conquer or control, judge or manipulate, but somehow celebrate it all as part of the plan of the universe. For each day we are becoming more of a global community. We have to see ourselves as a community when we deal with religious differences. Religion is rooted in an experience of the transcendent. Human beings experience *something*, which Rudolf Otto described as *mysterium tremendum et fascinans*. Religious beliefs and rituals are attempts to articulate that experience.[4] Why have people come to articulate very different understandings of God? Perhaps in our century we will come to a better understanding of the reasons.

There are many answers to the question of death. In birth, we become a part of the human race. We become ourselves, raw and growing, a self that is unique, unfinished. No matter how insignificant I may appear to be among the masses of humanity, I experience myself as important. My life means a great deal to me. Somehow, I cannot accept that my whole existence ends in death. It takes too much effort, work, and struggle to become someone, to take my place in the universe, for me to believe that death ends it all. What an incredible struggle it is to define myself apart and in contrast to others. It is the natural course of things to want to be in communion with others but not to be subsumed and consumed by them. This divine spark of transcendence within us is the starting point for a destiny that is not limited to earthly existence. For me, death brings to an end our history as earthly creatures. Why death? It seems to be a part of the natural order. Our human bodies are subject to aging. And the tasks of life are limited and achievable. Eternity could not be contained in the ordinariness of human life.

The will to live beyond death, the primitive instinct for survival, the longing for life without end runs strong and deep in my veins. In the tradition of Catholic thought in Western culture, there has been a lengthy discussion of the nature of the human will. The human person, often described as head, heart, and will, desires and longs for life. That appetite is open-ended and, in a way, limitless. Maurice Blondel sensed that within our will is a "primordial will" that pulls us into life, dreams bigger dreams than we could otherwise imagine, that calls and coaxes, inspires and pushes us to live. It is not that the human person becomes infinite through his or her desire, but rather that the desire is bottomless. The more deeply the human person plunges into life, into the relationships of marriage, family, community, and beyond, the greater the longing for life, love, and fulfillment becomes. In fact, Blondel thought it was idolatry to attempt to satisfy the will's endless desire with a finite object. For him, spiritual development enabled individuals to harmonize their own free will with this power of life within. This power can be symbolized by the beating of our hearts, the pumping of our blood, the inner workings of our organs and cells, which pound away every day, waking and sleeping.

I awake to the reality that I am alive, that I have been brought into life by a force outside of myself. I did not choose to be born, as Blondel stated. Something outside of myself has called me into existence. Sharing in the mystery of life includes the mystery of my longing for eternity. It does not feel absurd. It feels comfortably familiar.

Suffering

There are many endings in life, and death could be just one of them. Yet it looms before us, filling us with dread. The root of our anxiety must somehow be a commentary on life itself. What is it about human existence that throws us into such anguish? Life is full of suffering. And suffering seems meaningless. We can't see the value in our own lives, and we wonder about God. It seems clear that death alone is not the issue; it is the experience of living and the problems that we encounter that we must deal with.

What is suffering? In Chapter 1 we made a distinction between physical and psychological pain, between broken bones and cancer. We discussed emotional and mental anguish brought on by complex experiences, such as personal failures, regrets, the loss of love, fear, and betrayal. Pope John Paul II terms this kind of suffering "pain of the soul."[5] We rage against suffering that is brutal and intentional. We cry out to God for help. At the heart of our pain is this tremendous power of the spirit to stand outside of the experience and judge it as unworthy. Moral outrage reveals the depth of God's presence within us.

John Paul II points to Saint Paul's writings on the meaning of suffering. Christians stand with Christ in confronting evil and allowing life to spring forth when they suffer with Christ. Their suffering helps to transform the world, to bring about the kingdom of God.[6] When people suffer unjustly, thought Saint Paul, their innocent suffering has the power to transform, to bring them spiritual strength and solace, and to conquer the oppressor with a greater force than evil, that is, the power of love.[7] At the heart of the gospel is the fundamental reality that love is stronger than death and evil. John Paul II goes on to point to

Paul's statement in Colossians 1:24: "In my flesh I complete what is lacking in Christ's afflictions for the sake of his body, that is, the church."[8] The path through suffering to peace and healing was created by the death and resurrection of Christ. The reign of God was renewed by Christ not through glory and power but through humility and suffering. By taking up his own cross, Paul became a true disciple of Christ. Somehow human beings share in the divine mystery of redemption. Not through death on a cross—although innocent people die in such a brutal manner every day—but rather through their faith and acceptance of the power of suffering to transform. By following Christ the people of God continue to bear witness to the presence of God in their lives and to their faith in a God who saves. As he concludes his essay, John Paul II states:

> At one and the same time Christ has taught man to do good by his suffering and to do good to those who suffer….This is the meaning of suffering, which is truly supernatural and at the same time human. It is supernatural because it is rooted in the divine mystery of the redemption of the world, and it is likewise deeply human because in it the person discovers himself, his own humanity, his own dignity, his own mission.[9]

Life in the face of death necessitates a personal stance on the question of suffering. When I encounter the raw inhumanity of life, when I see people trapped by poverty in city slums, when I see the bruises on the face of a woman who has been beaten by her husband, when I stand in the emergency room and look at the body of a child who was an innocent bystander killed in a gang dispute, I see a world of human suffering. Lives cut short, chaos overpowering sanity. I have walked through Auschwitz, and I could still hear the cries of anguish. My response? I begin to pray. I raise my hand to God, to unite victim and creator. I speak the words of ancient prayers. I let my emotions wash over me. I have stood at the Western Wall in Jerusalem and let the tears stream down my face. The words of John Paul II make sense to me. Human suffering leads us into a world of transcendent meaning. We transform the chaos by the way we respond to suffering, our own suffering and that of others. Poverty, violence, and persecution demean the very humanness of existence, and I know I must reach out to people who have been marginalized, attacked, and vilified. The risks we take to help others, our willingness to embrace the other's suffering as our own, are a test of our character. In the face of suffering we need to exercise the virtues of courage and compassion.

I also see the brokenness of my own life. I have been victimized by others' prejudice, ambition, and needs. I have dreams that lie unfulfilled. Loneliness and worry have been frequent companions. And as I get older, the chance to turn my life around diminishes. Some things that are broken will never be fixed. I wrestle with the blessings and freedom I have enjoyed, knowing that my life on earth has been filled with material comforts and incredible experiences that few will ever know. So even my own happiness strikes a chord of remorse. I stood by helplessly as I watched my mother's body slowly destroyed by cancer. And now I see my father quickly aging and growing infirm. The struggles, emotional hurts, and physical pains of my children are at times excruciating to observe. I know now that primitive animal instinct to protect one's young.[10] And the pain of loving someone.

When it is close to home, when pain strikes deep within the core of one's soul, more is needed than courage and compassion. For me to survive and endure what life hands me, or what I have chosen freely and purposefully, I need an inner core of both self-love and self-sacrifice. When I talk with a woman who is existing in a violent relationship with a boyfriend or a husband, inevitably I find there is a hole in her heart where love for herself should be. When others hurt and oppress, confuse and disappoint, the heart must find a way to endure. Finding love within ourselves is central to living with suffering. I believe it is that "willing will," that force of life that grounds the transcendent nature of human existence, which is the font of love on which we draw. We love ourselves because we were loved first into existence. When I am hurt, I need to reach out and find a way to give life to myself again. And yet, in the midst of suffering there is a brokenness that cannot be fixed in this human life. I must admit that some of my dreams will never be fulfilled. Through a spirituality of suffering, I learn to let go. I have to grieve in order to find peace with my life. Grief is an honest response to life's heartbreaks. I know that my life should have been better. But I can live with what has happened to me. In a spirit of self-sacrifice I can accept that ordinary human life is limited, fragile, and inadequate.

So much is at stake in being able to live well. Perhaps that is why we value people who have come to grips with the challenges they face. We call them wise. Knowledge through experience is critical to personal maturity. It takes strength and self-discipline to exercise the virtues of courage and compassion, as well as to create a delicate balance between self-love and self-sacrifice. If there is any meaning at all in our being made in God's image and likeness, then we must grow wise. Yes, bless the children for they are innocent. But human life seems to beckon us to grow up, grow stronger, grow wiser. Failure and disappointment help to strengthen us. Hope is the energy that enflames our desires and spurs us toward the future. [11]

Although I can accept the suffering in my own life, the magnitude of human destruction raises larger questions of meaning. Why is it that God created this kind of world in which human beings wreak havoc on innocent lives? Where is God in human suffering?

Jesus on the Cross

In Chapter 2 we explored ways to think about God in the face of human suffering. How can a perfect and all-powerful God permit evil? It is not surprising that this question has followed us through the millennia—from the laments of Qoheleth, which biblical scholars date at approximately 300 B.C., through the early church fathers such as Irenaeus (c. A.D. 200) and Augustine (c. A.D. 400), to the present-day arguments presented in *Encountering Evil*. In a way, I would say yes to all of the choices they present.

God does not exist. Not believing in God is like holding our breath. We can do it for a few short minutes, but soon it becomes impossible and life-threatening to continue. It is also painful and unnatural. There may have been times when we thought God could not possibly exist. And yet, in my own experience, I have found that I cannot sustain this position for long. Life is too exciting, too sweet, too comfortable. We catch ourselves enjoying the sweet smell of the pine trees as we walk along a path, laughing at the antics of kids playing in a pool, making love, hearing a song that is so beautiful it makes our skin tingle. When we stop holding our breath, it is quite possible to believe in God. In fact, it comes naturally.

This does not change the fact that our expectations of God may not be accurate. It may well be that we have believed in a fictitious God, a God of our own making. This God protects us from harm, like a charm safely tucked in our back pocket. This God does not challenge us to take risks or to give ourselves to others. The tragedies of life teach us lessons we may not want to learn. Certain gods don't exist, we discover, and that may be a source of true regret.

God is not responsible for evil, human beings are. Ultimately, God is responsible for evil. How can we say otherwise? The world is completely God's creation. The ability to do evil was incorporated into the makeup of human nature. I agree with Maurice Blondel when he says human beings do not choose to be born and that we discover we are alive as we move in ever-widening circles of consciousness. The story of Adam and Eve does not explain the origin of evil. The punishments of pain and death are not consistent with the crime. It is a myth, a meaning-making tale that identifies human culpability. Do greed and envy destroy the goodness of life? Absolutely. Have human beings desired to be gods? Yes. Does our desire to lord it over others damage the carefully woven fabric of human relationships and community? Yes, again. So, it is not that the story of Adam and Eve does not express truth, for it does. But it is a mistake to mis-direct the onus of responsibility.

The more pertinent question, then, is why does God permit evil? Saint Augustine argued that human beings have free will, the ability to make autonomous moral decisions, and in fact the moral order depends on holding human beings fully and solely accountable for their individual actions. Without free will, human beings are God's puppets, marionettes on strings that God can pull at will to make or unmake any action. But people are not puppets. I haven't felt any strings. There is overwhelm-ing evidence that human beings act freely, without God's control or intervention. Augustine's defense of free will as the explana-tion for the perpetuation of evil has value. But it does not fully explain all evil. Earthquakes, floods, cancer, AIDS—these are matters that cause enormous suffering and fall completely out-side of human power. We can intuit human moral responsibility, and we can see it as a gift, a power to create lives that offer us a share in the divine nature of God as creator. It is the platform from which all that we do springs. And if we use it badly, then we should be challenged.

God allows evil so that human beings can grow. Following Saint Irenaeus's principle that we are made in God's image and we have to grow into God's likeness, the argument is made that evil is permitted by God to give us the greatest freedom and room for growth. Our divine destiny necessitates constant efforts to transform our human existence and to prepare ourselves for union with God. There is a purpose to the progression of life, from childhood to old age. The joys and successes of ordinary life, marriage and family, work and community, are more than ends in themselves; they are the stage on which we play out our earthly dreams and open our minds, hearts, and souls to the divine presence that will pull us into eternity. The bitter struggles of life, the wrestling with one's soul, the hard climb toward moral perfection through adversity and challenge, these create our moral fiber, help us to respond to God's call.

Saint Irenaeus's voice from the third century still resonates today. The stage of human life, empty and open, full of possibilities, beckons. I can sense a growing strength within me, allowing me to endure hardships, deprivation, and loss, and challenging me to rise to greater levels of love and self-gift. The movement toward wisdom is achieved through perseverance. A life of total ease quickly becomes a life without purpose. It seems credible that evil is a byproduct of human autonomy and power. Even the choice between two goods involves loss. I can accept the world as it is. Except for one thing.

God must be challenged, God-against-God, in protest. For John Roth, it is the magnitude of evil that begs the question of God's responsibility. No parent would freely agree to the amount of human misery that exists for the sake of their child's moral growth. Brutal mass destruction and starvation cannot be justified, and should not be justified. The remaining problem of evil is that it provokes a sense of meaninglessness. We can embrace challenge and struggle if they achieve a higher purpose. But what if no purpose can be found in the suffering? What if it means senseless annihilation before any moral growth or fulfillment occurs? For Roth, we must stand against God in upholding the ideals on which our whole moral order is based. Moral outrage is the response.

It may seem that we are on shaky ground if we start getting angry with God. A colleague told me a story years ago. She was working in an emergency room as a nurse, and a patient was brought in yelling and raging against God for his miserable situation. She noticed that the nurses around her hesitated, and she sensed that they did not want to get too close to him or touch him. All of a sudden it occurred to her that they were afraid. They were afraid of God's response.

The tradition of the Old Testament expresses a great range of emotions as Israel wrestled with its relationship with God. The psalms express joy, fear, anger, despair, triumph, loneliness, and anguish. Job stands in direct conflict with God over the meaningless of his suffering. The spirituality of our Christian tradition also finds Jesus railing against the fate of his friends and followers. The whole story of the Judean-Christian experience of God is rooted in a living relationship with a God who has saved, a God who has heard the cry of the poor, a God who has given life, beauty, and freedom. This living relationship produced the union of God and human person in Jesus. Our experience of the goodness of life fires our moral outrage at evil.

On whom should we turn our rage? On the perpetrators of evil. Fear of the Lord is the beginning of wisdom. But if we vent our anger at God, we may discover a path. The issue is our response— How do we respond to sinfulness? As a Christian, I return to the cross. God stands with us in suffering, has suffered for us. Perhaps it is God's outrage I feel inside of me and not merely my own. The reality of evil remains a mystery that threatens to overwhelm me. Will an answer be forthcoming? Until it appears, what remains is the question of action. How will I respond to the evil I experience in my own life, in the lives around me?

There is power in turning toward love, toward healing and comfort, toward courageous outrage. If we express no anger, at

God or at ourselves, then we allow evil to prevail. We can choose faith. We can choose to believe in the God who is revealed in the life, death, and resurrection of Jesus. In the world in which we live, we can fight evil or ignore it, we can excuse it, we can be defeated by it. I do not choose to be defeated by evil. Nor do I choose indifference. The compassionate suffering God on the cross shows me the path I will take.

Our reflections on the reality of human suffering move from questions about God's responsibility for evil back to ourselves. Wondering why God permits evil does not absolve us from action. Our own sinful thoughts and actions, and the destructive ways of the world, beg for a response. What will it be? In my mind, the issue of accountability comes to the foreground.

Accountability

Chapter 3 focused on moral accountability. We defined the notion of conscience as a fundamental precept on which to build an understanding of a moral standard. Human beings have the capacity to judge the value of their own actions and the actions of others. Societies construct codes of conduct, laws that instruct and guide the inner workings of community life. We hold ourselves accountable for our actions and legislate consequences for misconduct. The lived reality of these simple principles is flawed, of course. Historians have charted significant changes in the moral consciousness of Western societies, for example, the end of slavery and the growth of democracy. As we compare and contrast Western cultures with the larger, complex world, there are notable differences in moral codes and expectations. From within my cultural context (the United States at the beginning of the twenty-first century) and my religious worldview (an Irish American Catholic lay woman theologian), I see the basic moral questions as the only ones we are addressing in this project of constructing a personal theology in the face of the enormous mysteries of life and death.

I remember standing in Grant Park in downtown Chicago on a warm summer evening, listening to the evening prayers of a group of Buddhist monks and waiting for the Dalai Lama to speak. He had come to Chicago for the World Council of Religions meeting. The sounds of their prayers rose clearly, bumping in odd patterns into my eardrums, confusing and dissonant to me. When the Dalai Lama first spoke, it was through a laborious and slow process of translation. At a certain point he began to laugh, and then he spoke in English. I remember laughing, too, enjoying the breakthrough in communication. He said, "I am a human being, just like you." We have more in common than it first appears, he intimated. Across religions, genders, cultures, life experiences, the Dalai Lama and I could understand each other. As human beings we share commonalities. In our work of building theological insights, differences stand. The world is far too complex a place to think otherwise. But I must live and act from my own reality. From within the Catholic tradition, and its salvation story in time and history, I would like to speak about the end of life, about death and judgment.

I think we still cling to a belief in temporal retribution. We long for the good to be happy, healthy, strong, and to have life unfold in a gentle and prosperous manner. When we experience pain and hurt from the destructive ways of others, we long for some kind of punishment for them and vindication. Even our system of laws presumes that people will be held accountable in this life for their crimes. The goodness and possibilities of life are so apparent, and we long for a life filled with happiness. The dramatic flaws and limits to our fulfillment at times are heartbreaking and intolerable. Envy and greed produce ugly fruits. Wishing for the life of another lends itself to grasping judgments of moral worthiness. He has no right. She has no right. And the misery of others causes its own distress. How can I avoid the life she has? How can I escape his fate?

One of the stranger expressions of this is Shirley Jackson's short story "The Lottery." A group of people in a small town gather excitedly and nervously for the annual lottery. As the story unfolds, the reader discovers that the "winner" of the lottery is to be stoned to death. "The Lottery" expresses in story form a line of John Donne's: "Don't ask for whom the bell tolls, it tolls for thee."

The scarcity of resources, the inequities in natural and culturally produced gifts, creates a world that does not provide the same life, the same opportunities for all. For some people, life is a constant struggle. For others, life is a golden journey. We hold onto the idea of temporal retribution in an attempt to make sense of an unjust world. People who are happy deserve to be. And people who are miserable are somehow responsible for their fate.

We explored the spiritual and moral awakenings of Job, an innocent man who struggles to interpret the enormous suffering inflicted on him. Through his experience Job comes to compassionate understanding and communion with others who are suffering. In particular, as Gustavo Gutiérrez notes, he comes to stand with the poor.

The Gospel of John contains a healing story of Jesus with a man born blind; "His disciples asked him, 'Rabbi, who sinned, this man or his parents, that he was born blind?' Jesus answered, 'Neither he nor his parents sinned'" (John 9:2–3). Within the context of a transformed understanding of human nature, life, and destiny, Jesus tried to dismantle these moral judgments. He defended the innocent; even a woman caught in adultery was rescued by him. The society's stance of rigid judgment ran counter to the loving and merciful presence of God embodied in Jesus. In a spirit of love and forgiveness, Jesus reached out to sinners and victims to bring them healing and renewed community life.

In order to chart a course through the very difficult questions about judgment at the end of life, about purgatory and hell, our starting point is critically important. We need to take on a spirit of charity and tolerance, a spirit of humility and self-sacrifice. Envy and greed blind us. Vengeance is terrible. In studying Western art and literature, religious teachings and their history, it has become apparent to me how often human beings have projected their own vindictive desires and unfilled ambitions onto others. In Chapter 3 on purgatory and hell, there is ample evidence of distortion and lasciviousness in human expressions. As Dante describes his journey through hell and purgatory in *The Divine Comedy*, he happens to see some of his enemies. This seems a bit self-serving to me. The sexual perversity displayed in some Western paintings portraying hell, and particularly those that portray women subjected to unnatural sexual acts, suggests the suppressed sexual desires of artist and audience more than anything else. And the witch hunts in Europe and the United States again victimized women. These examples should sober our thinking about the claims that have been made about the nature of hell.

Theologically, we have inherited traditional beliefs about the workings of Satan and devils, personified embodiment of hell's creatures, and teachings of the eternity of physical punishments awaiting sinners. The New Testament worldview incorporated these assumptions, and they persisted throughout early Christian history. We noted in our study that the persistence of hell may have been determined by its pastoral usefulness as a "deterrent" against sins and crimes. But I can't help but agree with Marie Huber's arguments in 1731 that the punishment of eternal suffering far overweighs the evil produced in human treachery in this life. What is appropriate vengeance against a murderer? What should be the fate of a man like Adolf Hitler, who brought about the death of millions?

The key to any determination about the nature of hell and judgment has to be by exercising the virtues of compassion, forgiveness, humility, and self-sacrifice. Otherwise, I believe, our understanding will fall short and may very well be as subjectively inadequate as much of what we have inherited in the tradition. Not only do we need to sort out what we mean by hell, having expressed concerns about the accuracy of the tradition's depictions of hell, but there are additional problems related to hell's geography. Where is hell? Classic descriptions of hell in the bowels of the earth seem incomprehensible today. And locating access to purgatory in the islands of Ireland and Sicily doesn't seem reasonable, either. The revised *Catechism of the Catholic Church* makes a formal statement accepting the existence of hell but offers no rationale. Rather, the only theological interpretation offered is that the only suffering for any creature that would matter would be eternal separation from God. That makes sense to me. If I try to live with compassion toward others, knowing full well my own failings, then I can see the possibility for God's forgiveness and mercy to reach out to every human being. And images of eternal torment do not convince me that God wills such a fate for human beings. I think that the worst fate would be annihilation, simply ceasing to exist and never enjoying the peace of heaven. A world of torture and misery for eternity, occupied by evil creatures, does not fit with the God of Jesus Christ.

Purgatory, that theological thorn in Luther's side, seems credible to me. In this life we see "through a glass darkly," and our quest for enlightenment and wisdom may fall far short of what is needed to make the transition through death into a new existence in harmony with that divine spark within us. A time or place of final transformation would allow us to move beyond ordinary human existence. Traditional teachings about purgatory had us believe that atonement for sins on earth took place in purgatory. That explanation was unacceptable to Luther, for it challenged the efficacy of Jesus' life, death, and resurrection. Perhaps the image of Saint Catherine of Genoa holds true, that a fire purifies the soul. We need not imagine that as a physical fire but rather fire as a symbol of transformation.

We are held accountable for our earthly lives, for what we have done and what we have failed to do, and we are chastised for human sins in human ways. We already experience the consequences of sin in our daily lives, and these consequences persist through death. If we have as our destiny union with God, then growing into God's likeness seems to be the challenge we must take up and carry throughout our lives. We are creatures, and I think God judges us as creatures, not as gods. It seems far more important to me to focus on the person who has suffered and turn to the question of whether healing, happiness, and peace are possible after life is over.

"What Are Midi-chlorians?"

When young Anakin Skywalker is brought before the Jedi Council, in George Lucas's *Star Wars: Episode I*, he is questioned by the Jedi knights to determine whether a high level of midi-chlorians is present.[12] Anakin asks Qui-Gon Jinn what midi-chlorians are. He responds:

"Midi-chlorians are microscopic life forms that reside within the cells of all living things and communicate with the Force."

"They live inside of me?" the boy asked.

"In your cells." Qui-Gon paused. "We are symbionts with the midi-chlorians."

"Symbi-what?"

"Symbionts. Life forms living together for mutual advantage. Without the midi-chlorians, life could not exist, and we would have no knowledge of the Force. Our midi-chlorians continually speak to us, Annie, telling us the will of the Force."[13]

The Star Wars trilogy sparked an enthusiasm in a generation of young people that has not diminished over time. As George Lucas continues to weave his tales of life forms in the galaxy, of the presence of a Force that is the source of life in the universe, it seems that his version of the future is more attractive and believable to young people than the ancient myths of the past, such as the Christian narratives set in the Greco-Roman world of first-century Israel.

Perhaps Lucas has done us a favor. In opening our eyes to the grandeur of the universe, and presuming that life exists beyond the planet Earth, perhaps his movies will aid us to imagine a world bigger than our own backyard. If Thomas Aquinas were alive today, with his brilliant mind and mystical sensibilities, would he continue to argue for the resurrection of a physical body devoid of sexuality and function, as he described it in the *Summa* eight hundred years ago? I doubt it. The geographical issues of the whereabouts of heaven and hell continue to be stumbling blocks. If there is a physical heaven "in the sky," with angels and saints surrounding the person of God and singing hymns of praise for all eternity, as depicted by Dante in *Paradiso*, why can't we see or sense the presence of billions of our ancestors? If hell is in the core of the earth, why haven't we found it? No wonder people look out into the universe for other answers.

As Christians, our starting point is the story of the life, death, and resurrection of Jesus. There is a power and a comfort in holding onto a tradition that is two thousand years old and that binds us even further, back to the beginnings of civilization in the Tigris-Euphrates river valley. What is new does not necessarily express the fullness of the truth of human life. As social beings, we share our lives together, and we share a common history as a human race. We need our past to know ourselves. In Chapter 4 we discussed in detail the teachings of Jesus about the afterlife, and we relied on biblical scholarship to look at Jesus' resurrection. The whole of Christian belief hinges on the acceptance of this profound mystery, that God became united with humanity in an earthly existence. And in the person of Jesus, God moved through the chaos of conflict and oppression and accepted death on a cross, tortured and abandoned by his followers. That was not the end of the story. The resurrection of Jesus is the central theme of Christianity, and it is a matter of faith.

"How can some among you say there is no resurrection of the dead?" (1 Cor 15:12) asked Saint Paul. The people of Corinth struggled with the notion of a resurrection, as did the people of ancient Israel. Modern-day theologians, such as Rosemary Radford Ruether, struggle with the notion of a self that moves through death into an afterlife, assuming that it is a vestige of male pride and ambition. It seems to me that we have to stand with Saint Paul and say that if Christ was not raised from the dead, then we are fools. He says if Christ was not raised from the dead, then we have lied, blasphemed God for making such claims, and we continue to be burdened by our sins and the misery of the human condition. If we are to be Christians, then the resurrection of Jesus must be our starting point (1 Cor 15:15–19). I know it is mine. Whatever we say about heaven and the afterlife, for me, must be built on this foundation.

The Beatific Vision

It would be good to return to a classic image of heaven, that of the beatific vision. Union with God after death is the destiny of the human being, and it is experienced in knowing, loving, and enjoying God. What does it mean to imagine heaven in those terms?

Knowing God. To know God means that some kind of self survives death. In order to know God, we must have a personal identity, with an ability to experience God. It implies that a transformed self persists through death. The nature of that self may be beyond our comprehension. We have a highly individualized understanding of the self in Western culture, and perhaps we focus too much on our own individual salvation. We might be bound as a human community in more intimate ways than our tradition has recognized.

French biologist Jean Calmes discusses human nature and our experience of space and time, as well as our experience of the relentless passage of time, moving forward never to be repeated.[14] But along with this linear experience of time, we also have time that comes to fruition and completion. Within that notion of the duration of time, he notes the existence of a common thread, an interconnectedness of all of humanity person to person with the transmission of genes. Our genes contain three and a half billion pieces of information, the heritage of the human race transmitted biologically. Calmes writes:

> The genes are actually the memory of life and they gather together all that is of value from the past. In this way, we as human beings who have inherited this long process of accumulation, we are genetically in solidarity with all living things, those who lived in the past as well as those who live today, for we all come from a common origin. The combination of genes which define our organism needed billions of years of evolution....It is also important to note, that the gene is far from a complete being; it simply represents the program of construction and functioning of an individual....Contrary to what one frequently believes, the essence of our body is not the matter of which it is formed, but the ensemble of biological processes and structures which are proper to it and assure the unity of its life. The pounds of matter which we possess today are there only for the moment to support our vital functions; they are exchanged incessantly, so much

so that there is no biological molecule...present last year
in our tissues that could be found there today.[15]

If our physical bodies, the material that we see, feel, and touch,
that we use to define ourselves, are only illusively permanent,
then perhaps the notion of a spiritual body like that of the post-
resurrection Jesus may be more applicable to our resurrected
state. What makes us who we are is not our physical existence,
for that dies constantly, but the common history of humanity
written in our genes and transmitted in communion with one
another, in intimate union. Perhaps in death we maintain our
ability to know, that is, our ability to be aware and experience,
in such a way as to allow us to be in the presence of God and
one another.

Loving God. The greatest joy in human life is the experience of
love. The passion and desire we have for our beloved, our fierce
dedication and abiding love for our children, these are the great
energies that inspire poets and artists. So many questions and
images of heaven revolve around our need to stay in communion
with those we love on earth. How can I be happy if I am separated from my beloved? Preachers comfort mourners by assuring
them that one day they will all be reunited in heaven. Loving God
must in some way reflect our deepest desires for communion and
love. For we know that not all people experience love in the
course of human life, and even loving human relationships fall far
short of perfection. We want and need, we cling to human
expressions of love. We know that babies who are not held and
comforted, nestled into the loving arms of another human being,
fail to thrive. Life is not human without love.

The bonds that we share as a human family inspire us to acts
of bravery and self-sacrifice. That same spirit of solidarity is
reflected in the Buddhist belief that even after having achieved
liberation from the cycle of death and rebirth, a being will stay
close to other living things trapped in the cycle of suffering. Karl

Rahner also wrestled with the question of where the soul goes after death. No longer limited by a bodily existence, Rahner considered the possibility that the goodness of the human person continued to exercise an influence on the world. Love is a mystery. Our loving God and loving one another are central to our life after death. As Christians we have experienced the love of God as a divine being, we see the centrality of God's own loving nature in the Trinity. Love is stronger than evil, that is our belief. Love is stronger than death. We have seen that power even in ordinary human acts of love for one another.

Are we bound to the earth after death? Any notion of pancosmic presence should be cautionary, lest we return to the notion of heaven in the sky and purgatory and hell in the bowels of the earth. God's love for us has called us into existence. That love is a mystery. We know it because we have experienced it. Where are the billions of people that have existed on this planet? If we open ourselves to the reality that we are more spirit than matter, as Jean Calmes asks us to do by considering our biological nature, then we need to consider the possibility that our human identity can come to fullness in nonmaterial ways. Heaven, it seems to me, is the communion of saints, the communion of the human race in ways that we cannot yet understand, in loving relation to God, who is both lover and beloved. And so we move to the last dimension of this beatific vision, the "stuff" of this heavenly life.

Enjoying God. We are searching the universe with telescopes to find signs of intelligent life. In a spiritual way we are also searching the universe to find God. "What will happen to us when the sun burns out?" my son asked me when he was nine. What is our destiny as a human race? Are we bound to the physical history of the evolution of the planets, and will all of human life cease to exist when the sun has spent its course? Now is the time to have faith in God. The world is vast, extending beyond our universe, and all we can do is trust in the loving presence of that life within us, the power that called us into existence. As a community we have experienced the presence of a loving creator who sustains us, comforts us, and heals us. We cling to what is familiar. Both Jesus and Saint Paul talk about the transformation of a seed as the image of the life to come. We are but seeds, and the world we know is the land, sun, water. We cling to what is familiar and resist the need to change. Perhaps for the moment, since the world is what we know, we have every right to expend energy and enthusiasm living life to the fullest. We can rejoice in work and family, the pleasures of food and companionship, the beauty of a sunset, the smell of cut grass. And then we will have to let go of this life and move toward the next.

The image of the beatific vision and the promise of enjoying God are ways to respond to the heartbreak and suffering of this life. A physical resurrection would allow us to enjoy physical healing and pleasure, to make up for all that was lost. That instinct touches our hearts, and we think of all the people we know and know about whose bodies have been malnourished, beaten, abused, and scourged with cancer, AIDS, and other illnesses. To dream of pure happiness for them seems to necessitate enjoyment in the flesh. But perhaps that is not the case. If we find ourselves in communion with God and with others, then perhaps pure joy and contentment can be achieved. For Saint Paul, the promise of heaven meant that "the trumpet will sound, the dead will be raised incorruptible, and we shall be changed. For that which is corruptible must clothe itself with incorruptibility, and that which is mortal must clothe itself with immortality" (1 Cor 15:52b–53). As we grow in our likeness to God, we take on an ability to suffer for others. Perhaps in our resurrected state, we will have the courage to accept that our suffering is over and allow that to be sufficient, and open ourselves to the possibility of a world without pain.

The beatific vision moves us into relation with God. Enjoying God might mean that we have successfully made the transition from human existence to immortality. Where is God? And where is heaven? We experience God in this world, this universe. That is our starting point. We are a community of billions of people. That is almost impossible to comprehend. And yet within each one of us we hold three and a half billion memories of the human race. Could my limited self touch each other person? Impossible. That communion remains a puzzle. Where and how we enjoy God is heaven. I am looking to the heart of life on earth and out into the universe to search for the answer to heaven. From what God has done so far, I see the power of life. And at least I see where I need to be, hard at work loving and healing in this life and preparing myself to let go of it for the next. I don't believe the human race will be lost when the sun goes out, but I don't claim to know what will happen either. Given the mysteries on which even the smallest living thing depends, the power of life seems strong enough to sustain us and to transform us into incorruptibility. Perhaps we hold onto a pancosmic presence until all of human life is ready for complete transformation. And in the process, we have been given the promise of happiness in the presence of God. Enjoying God expresses our belief that no matter how different existence is beyond death, it will fill us with joy. God and humanity together, that is our future.

Conclusion

Death is the horizon of this world, it is the end of my life's journey. That is certain. Having come to full consciousness of the inescapability of death, the remaining question revolves around the "before": How do I live in the face of death? In reflecting on the great questions of our lives, it seems imperative to me that we answer them to the best of our ability. Maurice Blondel felt that urgency; although we do not chose to live, we find ourselves alive and thrust into a position of making something out of our lives. Time pushes us forward, and not to act is foolhardy.

There seems to be enough evidence of God's presence, of the goodness of life itself, of the power we have within us to love, to change, to give and receive, to grow and become more fully human, more fully divine and wise. Even the shortest life has its own story, its own beauty. Every single human being shares in the story of the whole human race. We are like children, still. Emerging from the womb, coming to trust life, coming into our own individual identities, learning life skills and gaining knowledge—like children we have a long road ahead. If I know that one day my life will be over, which I now admit is true, then I can choose to live well.

The deeper we dig into life, the more unbelievable powerful and real it becomes. The further we look into the universe, the more mysterious it is. All our whys remain illusive. No wonder most of life is spent in adulthood. How could we stand to cope otherwise? The virtues that came to mind when facing suffering—courage, compassion, humility, and self-sacrifice—are really needed for everyday living. And to fully enjoy life and feel open to the future, we need to love ourselves and allow for intimate love of the other. Happiness awaits those who have the courage to live, and the courage to face death.

Conclusion

John-Paul Sartre writes:

> At least, you say, what if he were to go to a professor to his advice. But, if you seek the advice of a priest, for example, you have selected this particular priest, and so you already know, more or less, what he is going to say to you. That is to say choose a counselor and you are still responsible for your own life [i.e., because you are doing the choosing].[1]

As I end this set of reflections on the mysteries of life and death, I realize full well that Jean-Paul Sartre's caution has merit. When you choose the counselor, you have already decided what answer you would like to receive. As much as we would like to lean on the guidance of others, we still remain completely responsible for our own lives. All that we do has subjective overlays. Sartre's dedication to a humanistic perspective led him to argue that such heavy responsibility was really delightful, freeing. Heavy or light, the burden remains ours.

In charting the course of this text, in selecting readings and articles, it is clear that I made hundreds of subjective decisions along the way. What were the central issues? Whose voices needed to be heard? What should be included? Excluded? Ignored? From my starting point others might go a different route and draw different conclusions.

In this text I have not attempted to state what *the* answers are; rather, I have written about important questions that need to be raised about the meaning of life and death, and then I offered my own theological reflections. I have tried to show a way to respond to these questions from my perspective as a Catholic lay woman theologian.

This text does not have a surprise ending. I began the whole enterprise years ago, researching, writing, thinking, while I was in the midst of living and praying as a Catholic. Light has been shed on some issues, and I have a clearer picture of my own beliefs. But I would not say that this book was in any sense an attempt to make a non-believer come to faith. Faith was my starting point. Theology is faith seeking understanding. My efforts focus on helping people sort through the many complex theological issues and work through to a point of understanding and peace. This is difficult because our culture is so resistant to spiritual matters. Death is pushed far from view.

Vickie Lannie, an educator in hospice care, commented in a lecture that no one ever dies in a hospital. They disappear. Quietly whisked to the bowels of the building, where a hearse arrives to take the body away, they must disappear because they are a mark of failure. It is rare for an individual to die among family and friends, to appear in a natural state, to remain at home while others mourn. They are left in funeral homes to be chemically treated and cosmetically altered, and then kept at a distance until they are left at the grave, not even lowered into the ground until the family is gone. The artifice surrounding death in American society creates barriers to spiritual growth and understanding.

Researcher Myra Bluebond-Langner encountered a group of children hospitalized with leukemia. She found that these children lived in two worlds: (1) a public sphere of pretense, in which they functioned in a social order as "children," that is, as young people who had a future and would grow up; and (2) a private sphere, in which they secretly helped one another prepare for death.[2]

American Catholic theologian Terrence Tilley, describing the theological implications of her research, suggested that we all need a place for "truth-telling," a place where we can honestly address the fact that we are moving toward death, so that we may make a life worth living in the face of that reality:

> Yet like children dying, we also have a need to know the truth. If Christians believe that, as Jesus said to John, "you will know the truth, and the truth will set you free," (8:32), then the church must be a space in which the truth can be remembered, enacted, and transmitted. The church must be a space where the pretense of the profane can be left behind. The church cannot be closed to scrutiny, but it must be a space in which Christians can learn to live in open awareness of the facts that being born is the one incurable disease....The church must be the place where we together can handle the truths which we cannot acknowledge in the secular spaces of our world.[3]

Tilley suggests that the Christian community has the potential for providing a space to explore the spiritual realm of existence. Of course, that has been the traditional role for religion. But sometimes ordinary Catholic life fails to meet this need. Church life can be as death denying as any other human activity. Prayer and purpose can be focused on raising the young, putting in new air conditioning, building new schools, and preaching about moral values and tithing. In my experience over the years giving workshops in parishes, I have discovered a great hunger for spiritual discussions about these mysteries of human existence.

In response to that hunger, I have attempted with this text to provide something to use in meditation, in small-group discussions, in prayer and journals, that will help people come to a clearer understanding of their own faith life. It is my hope, too, that the truth will set them free.

Notes

Introduction

1. Selma H. Fraiberg, *The Magic Years* (New York: Scribner's, 1959).

1. Death

1. Carl Sagan, *Cosmos* (New York: Random House, 1980), 11–12.

2. Stephen Hawking, *A Brief History of Time* (New York: Bantam Books, 1988), 174–75.

3. David Filkin, *Stephen Hawking's Universe: The Cosmos Explained* (New York: BasicBooks, 1997), 255.

4. Ibid., 155–56.

5. Hawking, *A Brief History of Time,* 121–22, 174.

6. Ibid., 116.

7. Filkin, *Stephen Hawking's Universe,* 217.

8. Ibid., 156.

9. Stephen Hawking, "Imagination and Change: Science in the Next Millennium," March 6, 1998, Washington, D.C., a White House gathering for the new millennium, recorded and televised by CSPAN.

10. Of writers of the biblical period, Philo Judaeus is identified as a significant figure of the Jewish community in the first century: "[Philo was] born ca. 25–20 B.C. of a wealthy Jewish family in Alexandria,....[He] trained both in Jewish tradition and in Greek secular studies, especially philosophy....Philo wrote of the Logos (Word), a radiation from the One (God)

relating him to human beings; and Philo attributed to this Logos personal attributes of justice and mercy. Probably both Philonic and Johannine Logos are independently related to personified Wisdom (Sophia) of Jewish sapiential writings" (Anthony J. Saldarini, "Other Jewish Literature," in *The New Jerome Biblical Commentary* [Englewood Cliffs, N.J.: Prentice Hall, 1990], 1079).

11. Elizabeth Johnson, *She Who Is* (New York: Crossroad, 1992), 95. Johnson also notes the same conclusion in Elizabeth Schussler Fiorenza, *In Memory of Her* (New York: Crossroad, 1983), 189.

12. Tacitus, quoted in Donald Senior, *Jesus: A Gospel Portrait* (New York: Paulist Press, 1992), 11–12.

13. Harold S. Kushner, *When Bad Things Happen to Good People* (New York: Avon, 1981), 70.

14. John Hick and David Griffin, in their discussions of the problem of evil in *Encountering Evil* identify these basic categories (John Hick, "An Irenaean Theodicy," and David Griffin, "Creation out of Nothing, Creation out of Chaos, and the Problem of Evil," in *Encountering Evil: Live Options in Theodicy,* ed. Stephen Davis [Atlanta, Ga.: John Knox Press, 1981], 46 [Hick], 107 [Griffin]).

15. Hick, "An Irenaean Theodicy," 46.

16. Elie Wiesel, *Four Hasidic Masters and Their Stuggle Against Melancholy* (Notre Dame, Ind.: Univ. of Notre Dame Press, 1978), 60.

17. Ibid., 30–31.

18. Elie Wiesel, *Night,* trans. Stella Rodway (New York: Avon, 1958), 74–76.

19. C. S. Lewis, *The Problem of Pain* (England, 1940; New York: Macmillan, 1944). Lewis was asked by the BBC religious editor to give a series of radio talks about Christian faith, which he did from 1940 to 1942. Lewis is probably best remembered for his novels, *The Screwtape Letters, Out of the Silent Planet,*

Perelandra, That Hideous Strength, and *Till We Have Faces,* and his children's books, *The Chronicles of Narnia.*

20. Lewis, *The Problem of Pain,* 93.

21. Ibid., 83.

22. Ibid.

23. Ibid., 98.

24. Saint Cyprian, "On the Mortality," *Fathers of the Third Century,* ed. A. Cleveland Coxe, D.D. (United States: Christian Literature Co., 1886), 469–75, nos. 8, 9, 17, 21, 22.

25. Saint Cyprian, "On the Mortality," n. 22.

26. Saint Augustine, *The Confessions, in Basic Writings of Saint Augustine,* vol. 1, ed. Whitney J. Oates (New York: Random House, 1948), Bk. I, chap. I.

27. Lewis, *The Problem of Pain,* 103.

28. Andrea Bocelli, *Romanza* (New York: PolyGram Classics and Jazz, 1996), from "Per Amore" by M. Nava.

29. These events are chronicled in Walter Hooper, *Through Joy and Beyond: A Pictorial Biography of C. S. Lewis* (New York: Macmillan, 1982).

30. C. S. Lewis to Dorothy L. Sayers, in Hooper, *Through Joy and Beyond,* 143–45.

31. Nevill Coghill, "The Approach to English," in *Light on C. S. Lewis,* ed. Jocelyn Gibb (New York: Harcourt Brace Jovanovich, 1965), 63, quoted in Hooper, *Through Joy and Beyond,* 146–47.

32. C. S. Lewis, *A Grief Observed* (New York: Seabury, 1961), 7.

33. Ibid., 26.

34. Ibid., 41.

35. William Nicholson, *Shadowlands* (New York: Penguin, 1990), 100.

2. Suffering

1. Stephen Davis, "Introduction," in *Encountering Evil*.

2. Stephen Davis, "Free Will and Evil," in Davis, *Encountering Evil*, 74.

3. Saint Augustine, "The Enchiridion on Faith, Hope, and Love," in Oates, *Basic Writings of Saint Augustine*, vol. 1, chaps. XXIII, XXVI, and XXVII.

4. Ibid., chap. XXVII.

5. Saint Augustine, "On Grace and Free Will," in Oates, *Basic Writings of Saint Augustine*, vol. 1, chap. II.

6. See the introduction to the letter of James in *The Catholic Study Bible*, ed. Donald Senior (New York: Oxford Univ. Press, 1980). Another proposal is that it is written by a follower of James between A.D. 90 and 110.

7. Davis, "Free Will and Evil," 69.

8. Alvin Plantinga, *God, Freedom, and Evil* (New York: Harper & Row, 1966), 58, quoted in Davis, "Free Will and Evil," 74.

9. Richard Woods, a Dominican priest and scholar, published *The Devil* in 1973, partially in response to the movie *The Exorcist* and other American movies and books about the devil. In this book he notes the ancient origins of demonology (see Richard Woods, *The Devil* [Chicago: Thomas More, 1973], 66).

10. David Van Biema, "Does Heaven Exist?" *Time* (March 24, 1997), 73.

11. For a summary of Jung's viewpoint, see Woods, *The Devil*, 79.

12. Hick, "An Irenaean Theodicy," 41.

13. Ibid., 42.

14. Irenaeus, *Against the Heresies*, trans. John Keble (Oxford: James Parker and Co., 1872), Bk. 4, no. 3.

15. Hick, "An Irenaean Theodicy," 41–42.

16. Ibid., 42–43.

17. Ibid., 46.

18. Ibid., 47.

19. Ibid., 51.

20. Ibid., 52.

21. Davis, "Free Will and Evil," 78.

22. John K. Roth, "A Theodicy of Protest," in Davis, *Encountering Evil*, 7–37.

23. Elie Wiesel, *The Trial of God*, trans. Marion Wiesel (New York: Random House, 1979), 133, quoted in Roth, "A Theodicy of Protest," 16.

24. Roth, "A Theodicy of Protest," 20.

25. Ibid., 35.

26. Griffin, "Creation out of Nothing, Creation out of Chaos, and the Problem of Evil," 105.

27. Ibid.

28. Wiesel, *Night*, 76.

29. Senior, *The New Catholic Study Bible*, footnote to Isaiah 52:13—53:12.

30. Kushner, *When Bad Things Happen to Good People*, 134.

31. Ibid., 85.

32. Ibid., 58–59.

33. Reeve Robert Brenner, *The Faith and Doubt of Holocaust Survivors* (New York: Free Press, 1980; Northvale, N.J.: Aronson, 1997), quoted in Kushner, *When Bad Things Happen to Good People*, 85–86.

34. Gustavo Gutiérrez, *On Job: God-Talk and the Suffering of the Innocent*, trans. Matthew J. O'Connell (Maryknoll, N.Y.: Orbis Books, 1991), 1.

35. Karl Rahner, *Foundations of Christian Faith*, trans. William V. Dych (New York: Seabury, 1978), 184.

36. Karl Rahner and Herbert Vorgrimler, "Hypostatic Union," *Theological Dictionary*, ed. Cornelius Ernst, O.P., trans. Richard Strachan (New York: Herder and Herder, 1965), 218. A more traditional definition of hypostatic union can be seen in the teachings of the Council of Chalcedon, which discuss "the union of

divine and human natures in the one person, or hypostasis, of Jesus Christ" (Joseph Komonchak, Mary Collins, and Dermot Lane, eds., *The New Dictionary of Theology* [Wilmington, Del.: Michael Glazier, 1987], 501).

37. Rahner, *Foundations of Christian* Faith, 181.

38. Thomas Hart, *To Know and Follow Jesus* (New York: Paulist Press, 1984), 24–25, 25–26, 26–27, 27–28.

39. Ibid., 34–35.

40. Jürgen Moltmann, *The Crucified God,* trans. R. A. Wilson and John Bowden (New York: Harper & Row, 1974), 276–77.

3. Accountability

1. Maurice Blondel, *L'Action,* trans. Oliva Blanchette (Notre Dame, Ind.: Univ. of Notre Dame Press, 1984), 3.

2. Ibid., 4.

3. *Pastoral Constitution on the Church in the Modern World, in Vatican Council II: The Conciliar and Post Conciliar Documents,* ed. Austin Flannery, O.P. (Northport, N.Y.: Costello, 1987), no. 16.

4. Ibid.

5. Gutiérrez, *On Job,* xviii.

6. Ibid., xvi. This image comes from the writings of Ignacio Ellacuría, a Latin American theologian who was martyred in San Salvador.

7. Ibid., xviii.

8. Ibid., 33.

9. Ibid., 87.

10. Ibid.

11. See Raymond Brown, "Apocrypha," in *The New Jerome Biblical Commentary.*

12. *The Book of Enoch,* trans. R. H. Charles (London: Society for Promoting Christian Knowledge, 1917), 46–49.

13. Alice K. Turner, *The History of Hell* (New York: Harcourt Brace & Company, 1993), 97.

14. Jeffrey Burton Russell, *The Prince of Darkness: Radical Evil and the Power of Good in History* (Ithaca, N.Y.: Cornell Univ. Press, 1988), 140.

15. This excerpt from the *Vision of Tundale* was selected by Jeffrey Burton Russell in his explanation of medieval images of Satan (Russell, *The Prince of Darkness,* 142–43).

16. D. P. Walker found this reference in a collection of sermons preached in Westminster Abbey in 1877 by Dean F. W. Farrar, (London, 1878), 66, quoted in D. P. Walker, *The Decline of Hell* (Chicago: Univ. of Chicago Press, 1964), 31. This follows two hundred years after a similar justification, voiced by J. Brandon: "Though a punishment be never so great and grievous, yet if it be such as the person punished doth deserve for his offense, it is not cruelty but justice. That wretched Villain Ravilliack…was…tormented to death in a fearful manner, yet I believe there were few honest men that every accused his Judge of cruelty" (*Everlasting Fire No Fancy* [London, 1678], 10, quoted in Walker, *The Decline of Hell,* 31 n. 2).

17. Walker, *The Decline of Hell,* 29.

18. Ibid., 4.

19. Russell, *The Prince of Darkness,* 162.

20. Ibid., 166.

21. Ibid., 237.

22. Matthew Horbery, *An Enquiry into the Scripture-Doctrine Concerning the Duration of Future Punishment* (London, 1744), 294–95, 305. D. P. Walker used this passage to illustrate his point about the "utility" of the eternity of hell.

23. For his discussion of the Enlightenment's treatment of the eternity of hell, see Walker, *Decline of Hell,* 3–70.

24. Walker, *Decline of Hell,* 37. For the Horbery quotation, see Horbery, *An Enquiry,* 207.

25. Walker, *The Decline of Hell,* 39.

26. Turner, *The History of Hell,* 195–96.

27. *Catechism of the Catholic Church* (Vatican City: Libreria Editrice Vaticana; Vaticana, 1994).

28. Turner, *The History of Hell*, 4.

29. Marie Huber, *Sentiments differents de quelques Theologiens sur l'etat des ames separees des corps* (1731), 404, quoted in Walker, *The Decline of Hell*, 42.

30. For convincing evidence of the development of the doctrine of purgatory, see Jacques Le Goff, *The Birth of Purgatory*, trans. Arthur Goldhammer (Chicago: Univ. of Chicago Press, 1981). Le Goff dates its official acceptance to 1274, at the Second Council of Lyons (237).

31. Ibid., 8–9.

32. Shepard B. Clough, ed., *A History of the Western World: Ancient Times to 1715* (Lexington, Mass.: D. C. Heath and Company, 1969), 307–8.

33. Robert Easting, "Introduction," in *St. Patrick's Purgatory: Two Versions of Owayne Miles and The Vision of William of Stranton*, ed. Robert Easting (London: Oxford Univ. Press, 1991), xvii.

34. See Le Goff, *The Birth of Purgatory*, 41.

35. Ibid., 42.

36. Ibid., 49–50.

37. *Catherine of Genoa: Purgation and Purgatory, and The Spiritual Dialogue*, trans. and notes Serge Hughes (New York: Paulist Press, 1979), 71.

38. *Catherine of Genoa*, 75. Interestingly, in the passage just above this she comments that "the suffering of the damned is not limitless."

39. *Canons and Decress of the Sacred and Oecumenical Council of Trent*, trans. Rev. J. Waterworth (New York: E. Dunigan & Brother, 1848).

40. Martin Luther, *The Table-Talk of Martin Luther*, trans. William Hazlitt (Philadelphia: United Lutheran Publication House), #DXV, from selections in *A Compend of Luther's Theology*,

ed. Hugh Thomson Kerr, Jr. (Philadelphia: The Westminster Press, 1943), 243.

4. Happiness

1. Dante Alighieri, *The Divine Comedy: The Inferno, Purgatorio, and Paradiso,* trans. Lawrence Grant White (New York: Pantheon, 1948), 129.

2. Donald Senior, C.P., *Jesus: A Gospel Portrait* (New York: Paulist Press, 1992), 40.

3. William L. Portier, *Tradition and Incaration: Foundations of Christian Theology* (Mahwah, N.J.: Paulist Press), 260–63.

4. Dermot Lane, *The Reality of Jesus* (New York: Paulist Press, 1975), 51–52.

5. Walter Kasper, *Jesus the Christ* (New York: Paulist Press, 1981).

6. Oscar Cullman, *Immortality of the Soul or Resurrection of the Dead?* (London: Epworth, 1958), 9–17, 25–26.

7. Ibid., 28.

8. Ibid., 9.

9. Origen, *On First Principles,* trans. G. W. Butterworth (London: Society for Promoting Christian Knowledge, 1936), 72–73.

10. Plato, *Phaedo,* in *Classics of Western Philosophy,* ed. Steven Cahn (Indianapolis, Ind.: Hackett, 1990), 73.

11. Tenzin Gyatso, *Freedom in Exile* (New York: HarperCollins, 1990), 10–11.

12. Saint Thomas Aquinas, *Summa Contra Gentiles,* trans. Charles J. Oneil (Notre Dame, Ind.: Univ. of Notre Dame, 1975).

13. Ibid., chap. 79, nos. 10 and 11.

14. Ibid., chap. 81, no. 14.

15. Ibid., chap. 82, no. 7.

16. Ibid., chap. 88, no. 1.

17. Ibid., chap. 88, no. 3.

18. Ibid., chap. 88, no.5.

19. Rosemary Radford Ruether, *Gaia and God: An Ecofeminist Theology of Earth Healing* (San Francisco: Harper San Francisco, 1992), 251.

20. Peter Phan states, "For Ruether, it is the symptom of the death-denying tendency of Western culture or, more precisely, of the male's desperate attempt to transcend mortality, to overcome his fear of death which haunts him as hunter of animals and killer of other human beings. It is ultimately an egoistic effort to absolutize personal or individual self as everlasting over against the total community of being" (Peter Phan, "Woman and the Last Things," in *In the Embrace of God,* ed. Ann O'Hara Graff [Maryknoll, N.Y.: Orbis Books, 1995], 214).

21. Rosemary Radford Ruether, "Eschatology and Feminism," in *Lift Every Voice: Constructing Christian Theologies from the Underside* (San Francisco: Harper, 1990), quoted in Phan, "Woman and the Last Things," 214.

22. Zachary Hayes, "Beatific Vision," in Komonchak, Collins, and Lane, *The New Dictionary of Theology,* 81–83.

23. Quoted in Hayes, "Beatific Vision," 82. Hayes also draws the reader's attention to Saint Thomas, *Summa Theologica* I, 12, 7, and 3, for Aquinas's discussion of the beatific vision.

24. Saint Thomas Aquinas, in *Introduction to Saint Thomas Aquinas,* ed. Anton Pegis (New York: Random House, 1945), Summa Theologica I.12, 1 and 6.

25. F. I. Boudreaux, S.J. *The Happiness of Heaven,* 4th ed. (New York: Catholic Publication Society, 1873).

26. Ibid., 18.

27. Ibid., 138.

28. Ibid., 200–201.

29. Ibid., 166–68.

30. Ibid., 178–79.

31. Hayes, "Beatific Vision," 82.

32. Colleen McDannell and Bernhard Lang, *Heaven: A History* (New Haven, Conn.: Yale University Press, 1988), 108–10.

33. Ibid., 109.

34. Ibid., 142–43.

35. Ibid., 144.

36. Jeffrey Burton Russell, *A History of Heaven* (Princeton, N.J.: Princeton Univ. Press, 1997), 22–23, 133–34. Russell states that "one concern of thirteenth-century scholastics was how, in the light of Aristotelian physics, heaven could be considered a place. ...Traditionally heaven had been regarded as incorporeal, but Albert the Great (1200-80), philosopher, theologian, and natural scientist, believed that it is a body, meaning that it is composed of matter. It is the noblest of simple bodies, a body composed of the highest element, fire. Or it is an essence beyond the four essences or elements: earth, air, fire, and water. The idea of a fifth, nobler state of being came from Aristotle through Dionysius. The scholastics called it 'quintessence' (*quinta essentia,* 'fifth essence')....[It] suggests some kind of corporeality, [since] it contains resurrected bodies. It is a pure body, with the qualities of splendor, immobility, and freedom from the natural laws governing the four-essence cosmos" (126-27).

37. Robert Hughes, *Heaven and Hell in Western Art* (New York: Stein and Day, 1968), 112.

38. Ibid., 111.

39. Karl Rahner, *On the Theology of Death* (New York: Herder & Herder, 1961), 22–23.

5. Life in the Face of Death

1. Rahner, *Foundations of Christian Faith,* 178–203.

2. Ibid., 181.

3. A friend of mine, visiting El Salvador in the late 1980s, read this statement on a banner at Sunday Mass. She was overwhelmed at the time, recalling all of the suffering and death that the community had witnessed.

4. Rudolph Otto, *The Idea of the Holy* (1917; New York: Oxford Univ. Press, 1923).

5. John Paul II, "Salvifici Doloris" (On the Christian Meaning of Human Suffering) (February 11, 1984), no. 5.

6. Ibid., nos. 22–27.

7. "But we even boast of our afflictions, knowing that affliction produces endurance, and endurance, proven character, and proven character, hope, and hope doesn't disappoint us, because God's love has been poured into our hearts through the Holy Spirit which has been given to us" (ibid., no. 23; cf. Rom 5:3–5).

8. The ambiguity of the meaning of this passage in Colossians is further evidenced by the note in *The Catholic Study Bible,* which reads: "**What is lacking:** although variously interpreted, this phrase does not imply that Christ's atoning death on the cross was defective. It may refer to the apocalyptic concept of a quota of 'messianic woes' to be endured before the end comes; cf Mk 13, 8.19–20 and the note on Mt 23, 29–32. Others suggest that Paul's mystical unity with Christ allowed him to call his own sufferings the afflictions of Christ."

9. John Paul II, "Salvifici Doloris," nos. 30–31.

10. The fierceness of that protective urge, oddly enough, was articulated by Saint Augustine as an argument in defense of war.

11. Methodist theologian John Cobb adds a postscript to *Encountering Evil* in which he states "the hope that makes life a blessing can take many forms, but all of them ultimately depend on belief in God. We cannot believe in God unless we experience life as a blessing. We cannot experience life as a blessing if we have no hope. We cannot have hope unless we believe in God. We need all three, and if we break the chain at any point, the whole will dissolve. We must not let our sense of outrage destroy our belief in the goodness of life."

12. Terry Brooks, *Star Wars: Episode I: The Phantom Menace,* based on the screenplay and story by George Lucas, (New York: Ballantine, 1999), 241.

13. Ibid., 241.

14. Jean Calmes, "Le Temps, La Duree, et l'Eternite: Reflexions d'un biologiste," *Bulletin de Litterature Ecclesiastique* 97 (1996), 259–73. Translation by author.

15. Ibid., 264–65.

Conclusion

1. John-Paul Sartre, *L'Existentialisme est un humanisme* (Paris: Nagel, 1970), 46.

2. Myra Bluebond-Langner, *The Private Worlds of Dying Children* (Princeton, N.J.: Princeton Univ. Press, 1978).

3. Terrence Tilley, "Dying Children and Sacred Space" (Wooniski, Vt.: Saint Michael's College, 1989), 16.